VOLUNTEER WORK

CENTRAL BUREAU
FOR EDUCATIONAL VISITS & EXCHANGES

LONDON EDINBURGH BELFAST

CONTENTS

Section V

PROFESSIONAL

RECRUITMENT

Section VI

OVERSEAS VOLUNTARY

SERVICE

ADVISORY BODIES

Section VII

VOLUNTARY SERVICE IN

THE UK & IRELAND

ADVISORY BODIES

Section IX

SHORT-TERM

VOLUNTARY WORK

Section X

INDEX

REPORT FORM

USING THIS GUIDE

This guide, the fifth edition of *Volunteer Work* aims to offer information, advice and encouragement to all those thinking about volunteering. It sets out to present a clear view of the wide range of options that are available and to direct potential volunteers to those organisations who can make the best use of their skills, time, enthusiasm and commitment. The term *volunteer work* can cover an enormous variety of activities, from spending a few years working on a development project in an Indian village to devoting just a few hours a week to conservation work in a local urban wildlife area. Perhaps the one thing that such different activities have in common is that they involve an element of service which brings rewards not just to the environment or locality in which the work is being done, but also to the volunteers themselves, in contributing to the enrichment of community life and expanding individual horizons and experience. To some extent the terms *volunteer* and *voluntary* can be misnomers, implying that volunteers give of their time and labour but receive nothing in return. In actual fact most of the placements listed here are paid in some way, whether by nominal pocket money or a wage equivalent to that of local workers; and accommodation is usually provided, sometimes on a half or full-board basis.

Volunteer Work focuses on long-term voluntary placements in the UK and abroad, with a time commitment of at least six months, although it does offer suggestions for shorter-term and more informal volunteer work. Most projects listed here are full-time and residential: volunteers live away from home, perhaps with other volunteers, often in surroundings that are radically different from those they are used to.

Section I To Be A Volunteer provides an introduction to the volunteering ethic, offers advice and information for those thinking of undertaking voluntary service, personal checklists to evaluate potential, a discussion of the key elements of being a volunteer, and what you need to think about before applying to work on a development project in the Third World. It also discusses the pros, cons and options of a period of voluntary service and includes details on opportunities for volunteers in developed countries.

Section II Understanding Development and Information Resources lists organisations who campaign on, and raise awareness about, development and development education issues, and are a valuable source of information, especially for volunteers going to, or returning from, the Third World. Suggested further reading and other useful sources of information covering voluntary work, development issues, taking a year out and travel are listed here under Information Resources.

Section III Preparation & Training and Voices of Experience covers preparation, briefing and orientation for potential volunteers, including what to expect of the sending agency and what needs to be researched on an individual basis, and lists organisations arranging specialist courses for those about to be placed overseas. Voices of Experience includes personal insights from past volunteers, who discuss their own experiences of voluntary service and give their impressions on how they felt the projects benefited themselves and the community they were working for.

Section IV Travel Advice and Returning offers advice on travel, health and insurance, and forward information on returning, including insights from returned volunteers on preparing for the reverse culture shock. Details of organisations offering advice on resettlement, reorientation and continuing commitment are also included.

Section V Voluntary Service: Recruiting Agencies lists organisations arranging volunteer placements in alphabetical order. Information is provided in a set format to aid selection and provide easy comparison:

Name and address of organisation including the title of any contact person to whom potential volunteers should apply.

Telephone number

Countries/areas lists the countries (or if in the UK and Ireland the areas) in which volunteers may be placed. In some cases the destination depends on the projects in operation during a particular year or is at the discretion of the organisation.

Profile A general description of the philosophy, aims and activities of each organisation.

Opportunities Details of the type of opportunities available, with a description of what work volunteers are expected to undertake. Where possible, details of the number of volunteers recruited each year are given.

Requirements Age limits for applicants, plus details of the personal qualities, skills, experience and qualifications that volunteers will require. Any language requirements and nationality restrictions are specified. Where applications from people with a handicap are considered, this is indicated as follows:

B Blind or partially-sighted
D Deaf or hard of hearing
PH Physically handicapped
W Wheelchair users

Duration Length of the placement, including any minimum and maximum periods. In general, *Volunteer Work* covers placements lasting from six months to three years.

Terms and conditions covers details of any costs to volunteers, hours of work, salary or pocket money provided, board and lodging, holiday entitlement, National Insurance, grants and whether travel and insurance costs are covered.

Briefing Details of any orientation courses held prior to departure or any debriefing at the end of the placement, plus information on in-service training or supervision, and language courses.

When to apply Applications and requests for information should be made to the organisations direct, and not via the Central Bureau. Early application is always advisable, giving time to prepare for departure. When writing to any organisation a stamped, addressed envelope should be enclosed, or, in the case of an organisation based overseas, an addressed envelope and two International Reply Coupons, available from post offices.

Publications Details of newsletters, annual reports and other publications which may be of interest to volunteers.

Section VI Professional Recruitment, lists those organisations working in development who, rather than looking for volunteers, recruit personnel with considerable skills, qualifications and overseas work experience.

Section VII Overseas Voluntary Service: Advisory Bodies gives details of organisations who do not themselves recruit volunteers but can offer advice and information for those interested in volunteering overseas.

Section VIII Voluntary Service in the UK & Ireland: Advisory Bodies details organisations who can offer advice and information for those interested in volunteering in the UK or Ireland.

Section IX Short-term Voluntary Work offers advice for those who are unable to commit themselves for medium or long-term voluntary service, or who do not yet have the necessary skills/qualifications. Details are also given of projects suitable for those who may wish to participate in a short-term project in order to gain some experience.

Section X Index and Report Form includes three types of index: as well as referring to the alphabetical index of organisations, you can also find a suitable agency by looking up the countries in which you would like to work or the type of project you are interested in. At the end of your voluntary placement, we would appreciate it if you could complete and return the report form, which will enable us to keep up-to-date records of the various organisations listed, as well as giving us some idea of volunteers' personal experiences.

Volunteer Work is published by the Central Bureau for Educational Visits & Exchanges, the UK national office responsible for the provision of information and advice on all forms of educational visits and exchanges; the development and administration of a wide range of curriculum-related pre-service and in-service exchange programmes; the linking of educational establishments and local education authorities with counterparts abroad; and the organisation of meetings, workshops and conferences related to professional international experience. Its information and advisory services extend throughout the educational field. In addition, over 25,000 indivdual enquiries are answered each year. Publications cater for the needs of people of all ages seeking information on the various opportunities available for educational contacts and travel abroad. The Central Bureau was established in 1948 by the British government and is funded by the Department for Education, the Scottish Office Education Department and the Department of Education for Northern Ireland.

Chairman of the Board: Anthony Carter
Director: Tony Male
Deputy Directors: Bill Musk, Graham Davey

Seymour Mews
London W1H 9PE
℡ 071-486 5101
Fax 071-935 5741

3 Bruntsfield Crescent
Edinburgh EH10 4HD
℡ 031-447 8024
Fax 031-452 8569

16 Malone Road
Belfast BT9 5BN
℡ 0232-664418
Fax 0232-661275

PREFACE

Our understanding of the role of volunteers has changed considerably over the years. In Britain, volunteering began in the late fifties almost as a natural follow-on from the period of national conscription which had just ended. Those leaving the forces with university places were obliging school-leavers to wait a year before starting higher education, and in order to put this resource of youthful energy to good use, school-leavers were encouraged to volunteer overseas for nine months or a year. A similar Australian scheme sent volunteers to Indonesia, and in 1961 President Kennedy launched the Peace Corps in the United States. The volunteering ethos took root and grew; early British school-leavers were joined by police cadets and apprentices. Volunteering was seen to build the character and in some cases to change the lives of volunteers, whether in their social attitudes or future career patterns. Their enthusiasm, hard work and commitment prompted public support and conveyed an image of the typical volunteer which has lasted to this day.

Priorities change though, and as volunteering overseas grew into its second decade the volunteer programmes of Britain and other Western countries had to adapt to the changing demands of their host communities. It became clear that the countries of the Third World had themselves no shortage of unskilled or unemployed people, and that what they needed most were professional expertise and technical skills which could be shared amongst their own populations. School-leavers were replaced by graduates and other qualified people, and more volunteers were expected to have a degree of work experience which could bring practical as well as theoretical knowledge to their overseas posting. The best qualification of all was seen to be the ability to train people and pass on one's skills to others, and consequently the demand was more for the specialist, technically qualified and experienced volunteer.

The third decade saw, with the Brandt Report, an increased recognition of the economic interdependence of the industrialised, developed North and the developing countries of the South, as well as challenges to the established views of *development* and *underdevelopment* and the part played by industrialised nations. To what extent were the educational and healthcare systems that newly independent countries had inherited from their colonisers perpetuating poverty and inequality? Were Western volunteers helping these countries' self-reliance or undermining their independence?

Once again there was a reappraisal of the role of volunteers and their relationship to the host community. Volunteer-sending agencies began to be more discriminating about the projects they ran and the organisations with whom they cooperated, making an effort to involve their host partners more closely in the work that was being done, choosing partner organisations locally based, with a knowledge of what work was really needed. There was also a move away from the idea that western technology could provide all the answers and a greater awareness of the need for technology and methods that were appropriate to both the local environment and host community.

What will the next decade bring? A quarter of the world's population still lives in poverty; almost a fifth is non-literate. The recent opening up of Eastern Europe and the need for these countries to rebuild their economies has revealed another skills shortage which volunteers can help to fill. The experience, skills and wisdom of an older generation, the retired executive for example, are increasingly viewed as valuable ones to share both with newly-emerging democracies and the developing world. Back in Britain, voluntary agencies are emphasising the need for development education, with returned volunteers playing a vital role in informing future generations and challenging popular myths and assumptions about the causes of underdevelopment.

SECTION I

TO BE A
VOLUNTEER

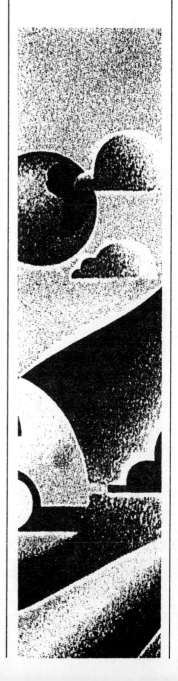

TO BE A VOLUNTEER

For many, the word volunteer conjures up the image of a young enthusiast working on a development project somewhere in Africa, Asia or Latin America. The volunteer could be teaching, training, nursing, distributing food, digging wells, building clinics, advising on agriculture . . . the list is a long one, but in some way she or he is assumed to be contributing to the development of the host country.

This section sets out to force self-analysis of just what volunteering can achieve - for the volunteer as well as the community, to challenge any myths and stereotypes that may exist, and to cover most of the pros, cons and options. In doing so potential volunteers should arrive at their own reasoned decision for volunteering, aided in their choice of agency, project and country, and crystal clear of their ultimate goals.

This section is to help you, as a potential volunteer, consider your motivation and commitment towards volunteering, to provoke you into thinking carefully about what is meant by *development* and to offer some insight into exactly what type of person the volunteer-sending agencies are looking for. Projects are essentially mutually rewarding and beneficial; both volunteer and co-worker are expected to be enriched by the experience of working on a common task and to have contributed positively, even if fractionally, to the betterment of mankind.

There is now a greater understanding that without the partnership and willing cooperation of agencies, officials and individuals in the country in which the projects are established, volunteers and indeed development aid generally may be distorting and harming the very development it is hoped to foster, and interfering intolerably with the right of the societies in question to determine their own destiny.

However, to argue as some have done, that volunteer aid for development is outdated and that such benefit as accrues from it comes in terms of personal experience for the volunteers, is to ignore the vital importance of personal contacts for the growth of mutual understanding and the transmission of skills. In this greater mutual understanding lies the best hope for a real improvement in the human condition worldwide. The witness of returned volunteers in their own community is or should be an important influence for change, without which mutual understanding will be increasingly replaced by self-interest and protectionism.

Motivation Your reasons for thinking about voluntary service may be many and varied, but whatever they are, they are definitely worthy of careful analysis. It is very important that you get at least some understanding of your motivation before deciding whether or not to volunteer, either at home or abroad. You must be absolutely clear, positive and honest with yourself about your reasons for even thinking about volunteering. All volunteers will share a certain amount of idealism, but a realistic expectation of what can be accomplished through voluntary service, and what you will return with in exchange, needs to be set down from the outset. Although rigid preconceptions are the last things expected of today's volunteers, some idea of what you are expecting, and why you are starting out from that position, needs to be examined. Which of the following, if any, apply to you?

☐ I feel voluntary service will give me experience and improve career prospects

☐ I am running away from unemployment/my job/personal problems

☐ I did consider volunteering in my own country, but going abroad is more exciting

☐ I have a political conviction/ commitment to the struggle of exploited people

☐ I have felt a call from God

☐ I am fed up of this country, I'm heading for the sunshine

☐ I honestly haven't really thought about why I am in a position to volunteer

Considering the importance of the answer, the question of why one is volunteering is often passed over by both volunteer and sending agency alike. You may find difficulty in answering; there may not even be a clear-cut answer, but the process of examining the reasons for even thinking about volunteering is a vital one. If you're considering undertaking a project in the Third World, for example, your understanding of why those countries are *underdeveloped* also needs careful examination:

Why are their people in need who have to rely on other people's voluntary actions?

How do the people of such countries come to be so poor, badly housed and underfed, and how can the expertise and investment of industrialised nations help?

One thing is clear: one or two years spent in voluntary service is a considerable slice of one's life and is far too valuable to waste. For such an investment of time and energy it is essential that there is a clear understanding of what volunteers expect and what is expected of them. Read through the following ten reasons for volunteering - some may strike a chord. You may not be prepared for the responses, but these are aimed at provoking you into really thinking about your commitment.

☑ I want to help the less fortunate

A perhaps well-meaning but rather patronising attitude. Have you given any thought as to how and why these people you want to help actually are *less* fortunate? What sort of help do they need, and how are you in a position to give it? In what way do you consider yourself *more* fortunate? Better off, better educated, more intelligent, in some way superior? Are these communities less fortunate in a cultural sense? If you are applying this reason to volunteering overseas, remember that Third World countries are no longer colonies. Perhaps you need to acquire some understanding of international citizenship and development issues. Perhaps a change of attitude is required.

 I'm sure they'd benefit from my technical skills and expertise

But are these appropriate to the conditions existing in the country where you will be working? The idea that Western technology can solve all the Third World's problems is a dangerous one. Hi-tech methods are not invariably the best ones, and may disrupt perfectly adequate systems that have been in use for generations. Will you be taking a course in the local language? Do you think you'll be able to communicate well enough to transfer your skills to the people that matter? Is the introduction of the technology going to have a material benefit in their day-to-day lives? Has it occurred to you that you will perhaps learn more than you teach?

 I want to show solidarity with the poor and oppressed

And presumably you want to work to put an end to poverty and oppression. Do some research. Is the agency you have in mind really working to change things, or is it just treating the symptoms, rather than the causes of poverty? Will the project you will be working on really benefit those who need it, or just help the elite and perpetuate an oppressive system? What kind of government does the country have, and what sort of Human Rights record? Couldn't you work for change far more effectively from your home country? What about the poor and oppressed

in the *developed* world - aren't they also in need of solidarity, or are you really just looking for the thrill of foreign travel?

 My life's going nowhere, I want a change, a break from the pressures of the rat race

Volunteering abroad will certainly be a change, but it won't solve your problems for you. If the rat race is getting you down now, will it be any easier after two years abroad? Running away from problems won't necessarily make them disappear. Nor should you consider volunteering to be an easy way out. And how do you feel you're in a position to help anyone, when you're in no position to sort out your own problems effectively?

 I want to do something worthwhile

Define *worthwhile*. What is it that you want to give or gain? If you expect to get immediate good feelings about setting the world to rights you may be disappointed. Volunteers usually take time to settle in and find out what is required of them. It may take several months before they feel they're making any progress at all. Many volunteers return home feeling that they actually contributed very little to changing the world or helping others, and that it is they themselves who have gained most from the experience.

 I'm having difficulty finding a job at the moment

Unfortunately, applying for voluntary work abroad is not the answer. Volunteer-sending agencies usually take on employed people with professional qualifications, and are not likely to be able to offer you a placement unless you have considerable work experience and appropriate skills. There are, however, many opportunities for voluntary work in Britain, which may help in giving you experience and proving to potential employers that you are a responsible and caring person. However, you need commitment to volunteer. It is not some sort of easy alternative to work; indeed, it requires all the skills and expertise of permanent employment plus more.

☑️ **I want to experience the culture and way of life of a far away country**

Very honest! Is a period as a volunteer the way to do this? How much have experienced the culture and way of life of another area or country whilst on holiday? Getting to know the people and what makes the country tick takes time and effort. Will you be living in the host community or in an expatriate compound which will remove you from the daily lives of local people? Even as a volunteer you may be considered to be in a position of power and authority - is this what you want? How will it affect your working and social relationships? How much do you know about the country already? Can you speak the local language fluently? How much chance do you think you'll get to become involved in the way of life and the culture whilst working? You will be working, not on some extended holiday. Do you have to go abroad to experience another culture and way of life? What about getting to know members of other cultures in your home country, including working to improve their lot in life?

☑️ **I'd benefit from the challenge and experience of working abroad**

You might benefit, but who else will? You may enjoy being thrown in at the deep end, but wouldn't you be of more service if you already had experience of voluntary work and

development issues? Perhaps you could consider working as a volunteer in Britain, or campaigning for a development organisation before trying an overseas placement.

 My western lifestyle has been very privileged and I would like to do something in return

It might also be considered a privilege to take two years out to travel to a far off country and work in the sunshine every day - not everyone can afford to do this! And watch out: this idea of privilege also has a patronising *West is best* air about it! Just how privileged is the lifestyle of other members of *your* community? Virtually all countries, developed and developing, have extremes of wealth and poverty, bad housing, illiteracy, high unemployment and immigrant or minority populations discriminated against on many levels. What do you do on a regular basis to help improve their condition? If you do consider yourself fortunate, there are lots of ways to give a little back, and volunteering abroad may not necessarily be the best one, especially if you lack the skills to contribute. Working for fundraising, campaigning or development networks at home can also bring results.

☑️ **The situation out there is so desperate, I've just got to do something**

Hold on a minute! First of all, what sort of skills have you got that can help? Sympathy and compassion are all very well but they alone can't change things. In cases of famine and disaster for example, the need is more for cash than people, so your energies might be better channelled into fundraising and working for change from home. How much do you actually know about how this crisis has arisen? But isn't the help you can offer only very short-term? What can you do on a long-term basis that would be more effective? And in the long-term, shouldn't people be given the chance to solve their own problems instead of being told what to do by well-meaning foreigners? Do we really have the answers?

As you can see, working out your motivation may prove complicated, but it is nonetheless important to try sorting out in your own mind both what you expect give to and gain from voluntary service, and whether these are realistic expectations. The most useful projects may come about as a result of the needs and the initiatives of people at the grassroots, where volunteers help those people develop *themselves*.

Janet Taylor has done two voluntary work placements for Christian Outreach, first of all as a mother, child and community health nurse on the Thai-Cambodian border, and secondly working as part of an emergency team sent out to run a therapeutic feeding programme for the Kurdish refugee community in northern Iraq and Turkey. She feels strongly not only that volunteers should carefully consider their motivation, but also that the aid agencies themselves should make sure that projects are really needed:

Whilst it is good and encouraging that people do volunteer to help those in need, anyone who feels that this is what they would like to do should examine first their own attitudes and motives for wanting to do the work, before applying to any organisation. An overwhelming desire to meet the needs of the people of the country is essential and should overlie all other agendas of an organisation and the people

employed by them. If the nationals you aim to help don't want a project/programme, or see no need for it, or are not included in the planning of it, then they will not work alongside you or be in support of the programme, which will lead eventually to the programme failing to achieve anything. To carry on regardless in this instance is a total waste of resources. In addition, any volunteer should be seeking to make his/her role redundant, replacing the position with a local who has received adequate training by the expatriate. This situation must always be preferable to having expatriate control of all programmes.

Janet explains that the project she worked on in Thailand is now being wound down. As refugees return to their country and as the existing national staff are now better trained, the number of volunteers is greatly reduced. The emergency programme amongst the Kurdish refugees was also closed down as, on evaluation, it was felt to be no longer necessary.

Qualifications and experience The days of agencies sending unskilled school leavers to work in the Third World are long gone. Although there are a number of organisations placing those taking a year out on worthwhile community schemes overseas (further information in *A Year Between*, see under the *Information Resources* section), volunteer-sending agencies now look for useful qualifications and transferable skills, usually backed up by solid experience of putting such skills into practice. Even recent graduates are unlikely to be placed as volunteers if they lack basic work experience. This is understandable: someone who has made the transition from being a student to working within the structured discipline of an office or work environment will have gained valuable management and organisational skills and will be better placed to organise their work in a new situation overseas.

Most agencies look for at least two years' work experience; others, especially those covered in the *Professional Recruitment* section, will expect applicants to have already worked in development overseas. If you lack experience and still want to volunteer you should first consider doing a voluntary placement in your own country. Alternatively, you could postpone volunteering until you have more experience under your belt - this has the advantage of giving you more time to consider the options, find out what specific skills are needed and get yourself properly prepared. The following tips may help you better plan any period of preparation for voluntary service:

Pick up some additional basic skills Learn to drive - in many areas this is an essential skill, as is a knowledge of vehicle maintenance. If you already hold a driving licence, try to get experience on a range of vehicles, including four wheel drive and minibuses. Take evening classes in administration and office skills such as book-keeping or typing, or practical subjects such as bricklaying or plumbing. The ability to turn your hand to a variety of tasks will always be worthwhile on a development project.

Go for breadth of experience At village level there is likely to be a need for generalists rather than specialists, so if your present job moves you around departments, take advantage of this to get as broad a training as you can. The more adaptable you can be, the better. Apply any skills you have to the benefit of your own community, gaining more practical experience and training.

Go for hands-on experience Look out for any chance to get real practical experience, find out how and why jobs are done in a certain way, find out how to do-it-yourself. The more hands on experience you get in doing tasks, the better able you will be to do them overseas, even if materials are not ideal and tools are missing. A knowledge of simple, practical jobs is likely to be most useful to you in the field.

Get experience of teaching Most agencies expect volunteers to transfer their skills to those around them, so start now by learning to be a communicator. You could perhaps help to run a youth group, volunteer to teach basic English, literacy or maths, or take a Sunday school class. Anything involving sharing and communicating skills and ideas is bound to stand you in good stead.

Learn about the issues The organisations listed in the *Understanding Development* section offer a variety of resources concerned with development issues. It is also worth reading up about development work in your own particular field, be it health, agriculture, technology or teaching. Getting involved in campaigning or fundraising will also be an excellent way of learning about the problems facing Third World countries and the means that exist to solve them.

Skills Working overseas on a development project will usually mean that you will have more responsibility than you currently have. The full range of your professional and inter-personal skills will be tested and developed, as you develop new perspectives in your chosen field. New in-service skills will have to be quickly acquired, in areas such as cross-cultural communications, project planning and adaptation on the ground. Time scales will have to be revised, particularly if the project you are placed on has not been in operation for long. It can take many years before the process of development can be measured within the local community, and as an outsider you may have even more difficulty in recognising the changes that have already taken place.

If you are going to transfer your skills to the host community, and share in what they can offer you, effective communication goes way beyond the boundaries of language proficiency. You will need to understand the various aspects of life in the new society, study the cultural background and be sensitive in developing and adapting to new situations. To many new volunteers the given level of independence and high-level decsion making can be as frightening as it is challenging. You may well be looked to for leadership and resourcefulness, and it will be through your imagination, determination and flexibility that will get the project completed at the end of the day. You will also be living and working in close proximity with fellow workers, and all your organisational and inter-personal skills will be put to the test. Your ability to adapt and cope with ever-changing situations will be the key to the success of your placement.

As you have an interest in the politics, history and culture of the host community, so they will be interested in yours. This may mean acquiring background knowledge of the political, economic and geographic situation of your own country before your overseas placement, as well as expanding your interest and in-depth knowledge of worldwide current affairs. This international component of your skills, the degree of your international and intercultural understanding, will be as valuable on your placement as your professional qualifications and skills.

Volunteering nearer home If you have no special qualifications, skills or experience, then opportunities to work on a development project in the Third World are now extremely limited. As well as the fact that these countries may themselves already have large numbers of unskilled, unemployed young people, it is also the case that most volunteer-sending agencies need to recruit people who can put specialist skills and experience into practice. Those agencies who do organise volunteer placements abroad for those without particular skills will generally expect them to raise quite a large sum of money to cover the placement fee, travel and living costs, viewing the placement not simply as a period of service, but also as an educational and cultural experience.

However, you don't *have* to travel far afield to find out about other cultures. Britain's population, for example, is made up of many cultures and many faiths, and there are plenty of opportunities to work with them. You could also volunteer in another European country or in North America.
Working to overcome the problems caused by disability, poverty, bad housing, illiteracy, unemployment or discrimination against an immigrant population presents a very worthwhile challenge. Or if you are motivated by a desire to work for world development you can do this in your own country - see the *Understanding Development* section for a list of organisations, many of which need volunteers to help with fundraising, campaigning or administration. Voluntary work experience in your own country may make it easier to be accepted as a volunteer overseas, quite apart from the contribution you can make to the welfare of the community with which you will be working. Jonathan Allat, a former volunteer with The Missions to Seamen, found that he

could work for the improvement in education, conditions and welfare of people from all over the world without leaving the UK:

I had hoped to spend a year abroad, so I was disappointed when I was posted to Southampton, but the multi-national, multi-cultural clientele at the Mission meant the world came to me. I spoke to British seafarers in transit to and from the Gulf War, Indians at the time of Gandhi's assasination, and Yugoslavians when their civil war started.

Many of the options for long-term voluntary work in western countries are in the field of social and community service. This can be a particularly valuable experience for everyone, especially those contemplating a career in health care or social work. Although the work is classed as voluntary, this does not necessarily imply that you work for nothing. Most placements covered in this guide are residential: board and lodging are provided, plus, in some cases, a certain amount of pocket money to cover personal expenses. Often, volunteers live and work together with the people they are there to help, and in order to promote a family atmosphere, emphasis is placed more on common humanity rather than on any distinction between volunteer and resident. The ideas and attitudes of voluntary service which used to be expressed as *helping those less fortunate than ourselves* or as *giving benefit to people in need* are now considered inappropriate and patronising. Volunteers tend to learn and gain a lot from the people with whom they are working, whether these are people with a physical disability, an illness, learning difficulties, a need for food and shelter, or simply difficulty in coping with the pressures of society. Despite the many rewards, this type of voluntary service can, at least to begin with, be both mentally

and emotionally draining. You will be in a very new situation, probably away from your home and family, living amongst people who may be demanding in a way you have not had to deal with before.

It is therefore important that you consider your own strengths and weaknesses before formally applying and discuss any doubts or questions with the people running the project. In all likelihood they will be able to offer a lot of training and support, but you will also need to be fairly self-reliant. The ability to take initiatives within the framework of the project team, to cope with crises, to exert discipline without being authoritarian, and to maintain a sense of humour and perspective, is usually essential. You may not be aware of possessing all these capabilities, but the training and experience provided by a period of community service may well bring them to the fore. This can only stand you in good stead and prepare you for any future challenges you may have to face.

Jane Manning worked for Cambridge Cyrenians as part of a team living at a direct access hostel for nine homeless people. Jane left in July 1992 and now works as a salaried worker on a housing project in Bedford:

I see my time as a volunteer worker as one where I used my abilities to assist people to improve aspects of their lives or to accept them. As a live-in volunteer the project had an aspect of family community that many residents had not experienced for many years. This made the residents feel more at ease talking to me and I was viewed less as an outsider.

In the six months I was at the project I found myself in an environment that was often challenging. Frequently confronted with new situations. However I feel that what I put into the work was a fraction of what I received back from it. I forged and maintain many friendships with the residents and in the local homeless population.

I would recommend voluntary work as a way of discovering parts of your own expectations in life and realising the hidden problems that exist in our society.

Volunteering from home If you've never done any voluntary work before and feel a little daunted by the prospect of committing yourself on a long-term residential basis there are still countless opportunities to volunteer in your home area. In its 1991 Survey of Voluntary Activity in the UK the Volunteer Centre UK defined voluntary work as *any activity which involves spending time, unpaid, doing something which aims to benefit someone (individuals or groups) other than or in addition to close relatives, or to benefit the environment.*

A very broad definition, which can encompass an enormous variety of opportunities. Put like this, even helping someone across the road can be classed as volunteering! It has been estimated that in the UK between one third and one half of the population devotes some spare time to organised voluntary work. So you don't have to be an extra special person with proven skills - *anyone* can volunteer!

Faced with such a wide variety of opportunities, the first thing you need to do is decide what sort of voluntary work is right for you. Your motivation might be political, environmental, humanitarian or religious; perhaps you have a desire to help other people, look after children, campaign for change, stop pollution, reduce poverty and need, care for animals or offer help in emergencies. Discover what it is that you really care about, and look for an organisation that has this issue at its heart.

You should also be aware of what it is you are good at and what sort of work you enjoy doing. There's no point volunteering to do practical work if you don't know one end of a screwdriver from the other. If you like talking to people then you might not be very happy stuck in an office doing the filing. On the other hand, if you're neat and methodical you may quite enjoy the administrative side of things. Everybody has their strong and weak points, and all types of people are needed to keep a voluntary organisation going: campaigners and lobbyers; people to offer support and friendship; practical people who like to be where the action is; counsellors, advisors and problem-solvers; clerical workers, administrators, secretaries, organisers and managers.

Ask around your local area to find out about voluntary organisations; check in your local library; consult the phone book, *Yellow Pages* or *Thomson's Directory*; or contact your local Volunteer Bureau. The organisations listed in the *Advisory Bodies - UK & Ireland* section should also be able to help you. Once you've found a voluntary organisation you would like to work for, ask to speak to the volunteer organiser, who will be able to tell you what sort of work is available. You will probably have to fill in an application form and attend an interview - this will help them to place you in work to which you are most suited. You may be asked to provide references, either from a past employer or someone who knows you well, just to confirm that you are who you say you are and that you'll be able to do the work. If you are going to be working with children, you may also be asked to disclose any police record. The interview is also an opportunity for you to find out all you can about the organisation and where volunteers fit into the structure, so don't be afraid to ask lots of questions.

As a volunteer, even though you may feel you are working fairly informally for no financial reward you still have rights and should not just be treated as an extra pair of hands or someone to do the dirty work. Volunteering is a matter of free choice, and your willingness should not be exploited, so don't feel pressurised into doing work you really don't want to do. Your hours of work should be agreed and put in writing - you have other demands on your time, and therefore should not commit yourself to giving more time than you can afford. You should have some kind of verbal or written description of the job you will be doing, and if the job is likely to change it is only fair that you should be consulted. Make sure you know who is supervising your work and whom you can approach to talk through any problems. If your work is likely to incur any expenses, find out how to claim these back; if any special clothing or equipment are needed then these should be supplied by the organisation, not by you.

You should be adequately insured by the organisation whilst at work, and as with all employees, you should not be expected to work in unsafe or unhealthy conditions. Above all, make sure that the work you are doing is genuinely voluntary - you should not be putting someone out of a job by doing work which was previously paid.

Volunteering should give you a chance to enhance the skills you already have and learn new ones, either on-the-job or in some cases through a training course. As your skills develop, so should your work, and like any job it should be reviewed at regular intervals. If you find the work tedious and unsatisfying, then make your voice heard and ask if you can do something that is more demanding or entails more responsibility. Remember, it's in everyone's interest for you to feel fulfilled and happy in your work, because then you're much more likely to carry on with it!

If you are claiming benefits such as Unemployment Benefit or Income Support you must inform your local payment office if you are doing any voluntary work. Payment of benefits will not usually be affected as long as you are still available for and actively seeking work. This means that you must be willing to give up your voluntary work at 24 hours' notice to attend an interview or take up a job, and that you must be able to show for each week you claim benefit that you have taken reasonable steps to find a job. Your local Social Security Office, Unemployment Benefit Office or Jobcentre should be able to give you advice and supply you with a copy of leaflet FB26 *Voluntary and part-time workers* which discusses the issue in more detail. If you incur any out-of-pocket expenses whilst undertaking voluntary work, such as travel costs, for example, the reimbursement of such costs will not affect the payment of benefits.

Obviously, residential voluntary projects will require more of a full-time commitment from volunteers than more informal voluntary work, and because of this you may not qualify for benefits as you will not be able to say you are actively seeking work. However, you will not be entirely without resources as most residential projects provide board and lodging and will supply volunteers with pocket money to cover basic personal expenses.

Personal qualities Qualifications and experience, however impressive, are no good unless a volunteer has the right personal qualities. To begin with, if you can't communicate your skills to, and learn from, other people, then you are unlikely to be of much use to any development project. The ability to make friends and get on with all kinds of people is vital. Volunteers also need to be able to show sensitivity and tolerance towards cultures different from their own, as well as enough flexibility, patience and humour to enable them to work with people who may be used to doing things in a different way and perhaps have a different sense of priorities. You may well find yourself in a more responsible position than you have been used to, with people coming to you for advice and treating you as an expert, so a considerable amount of initiative, confidence, self-reliance and decision-making ability will be required. Prospective volunteers should take careful note of the personal qualities required by the agency. How many of the following can *you* check positively:

☐ I get on with people

☐ I can work independently and show initiative

☐ I am prepared to learn from the community I will be working in

☐ I can work as part of a team

☐ I can bridge the gap between what the project will expect of me and what I am

☐ I can work the way others want me to work

☐ I am too used to doing things my own way

☐ I could learn the language

☐ I am adaptable and flexible

☐ I am tolerant and sensitive to other cultures

☐ I have got communication skills

☐ I am patient and tactful

☐ I am independent and self-disciplined

☐ I have a sense of humour

☐ I have a desire to seek challenges

Aside from the working environment, you may also have to deal with your own feelings of isolation and homesickness, not to mention strange food, the heat, weird insects, perhaps a lack of amenities. Luc Bertrand, who is UNAIS Field Coordinator in Burkina Faso, has experience of life in a small African village, and says it can be a strange and somewhat disconcerting experience for many project workers. Here he offers some insights:

If you have to live in a small village, you would do well to prepare yourself psychologically. There will be no cinema, nowhere to go out, and you may find it difficult to make local friends. Moreover, there will be little or no cultural activity and any intellectual exchanges will be at the most basic level.

Loneliness is one of the greatest problems faced by a project worker in a village. Unless you make friends with local officials or teachers you will find it an intellectual desert. You must therefore be able to adapt yourself to your surroundings, and cultural adaptability is a most important characteristic for a successful project worker.

When you first arrive you will attract a great deal of attention. The people living around you will be very curious and may appear somewhat intrusive. The way of life of a white person is very different from what they are used to; his or her possessions and how they are used will also be novelties. You need to accept and even expect visitors who will come to your home merely to 'be there' and not necessarily to talk or chat to you. From their point of view, the fact that they are there is enough. For a westerner, this can seem most strange, as receiving a visitor usually implies extending a welcome and therefore some kind of personal exchange, at least a conversation.

At the same time, the person at the receiving end of this strange experience has a need for a degree of solitude, or privacy. He or she has to integrate into the village and therefore requires time to take in all these new and disconcerting experiences.

For project workers living in this kind of environment, two or three days in a lively town once a month becomes an absolute necessity ... to eat different foods, to enjoy the choice of a thousand different leisure activities, to go to the cinemas, bars and restaurants - to experience the variety of urban life.

Coming to terms with cultural differences constitutes a major aspect of living and working in a new environment. If you've grown up with a certain set of beliefs, viewpoints and ways of working you may take it for granted that these are *right*, especially if they have never seriously been challenged before. Everyone has their own preconceptions or prejudices, usually determined by their upbringing and the social attitudes of the culture to which they are accustomed. In order to break down barriers it is therefore important for you to be able to see where your own assumptions come from and to try and understand and live with the way other people see things. It would be inappropriate for you to impose what may be a western, urbanised outlook on a completely different, rural community. Be open to differences, even if you think they are *wrong* - they have been developed over generations, are probably well-adapted to the surrounding environment and may teach you a lot about your own beliefs and attitudes. The following comments from a volunteer who worked in Zimbabwe are a good illustration of this:

Coming to Zimbabwe has shown me many things about my own cultural assumptions and habits of thinking and behaving. Things I used to regard as generally valid I now see, in the light of a quite different rural and communal way of life, as specialised and even odd social traits . . .

I came out with typical criticism of my project like there's no system to working, everyone spends too much time talking together in the office, or they come to decisions in such a roundabout way. It was just that I often didn't understand what was being said, or the significance of it, the relationships between people and the importance of showing hospitality. People joked about me always being busy, unable to spend time with them.

In agricultural work one day we were shifting earth from one place to another where trees were to be planted. All project members were working. The bucket chain broke down after a little while and everyone began to carry the buckets of earth from A to B in pairs or groups. I started to argue about inefficiency - the first time I'd expressed frustration I'd experienced in other situations, but of course I spoke up in work I thought any fool could organise (more fool me). Some workers just smiled, others were hurt and humiliated by my condemnation. One woman spoke up: We are not machines, *she said.* We are people. *And the work continued.*

The best way to gain an understanding of another society's customs and values is through personal contact. If you know which country you will be going to, try to get the chance to talk to a native of the country before you leave. There may, for example, be an immigrant community near where you live, or a refugee group. The cultural section of the relevant embassy may organise social events or put you in touch with a society for promoting understanding between Britain and that particular country. People are usually happy to talk about the way things are back home and you may learn a lot more from them than from reading books.

Which agency? The volunteer-sending agencies ask volunteers about their background, competence, views and intentions; volunteers have an equal right to ask similar questions of the agencies, and they owe it to themselves, the organisation and most importantly the people they will be working with to ensure that they are well-informed. You may be anxious to be selected, but remember that it is a two-way process; as much caution should be shown to the agency as they will show the potential volunteer. Talk to representatives, ask to see field reports and contact returned volunteers who can provide information based on personal experience. Make sure that your own motivation for volunteering does not conflict with the general aims of the agency

you have selected. Ask for further information about its background and philosophy, details of aims and objectives, its scale of operation, the type of enterprise, how it is run, and its support system both in the UK and overseas. The agency should be honest enough to provide you with details of the problems to be encountered, the projects that failed and the basic dilemmas still unresolved after years of activity, as well as their successes. They should offer their views on development and underdevelopment, and explain what role they feel volunteers have to play in this.

Which country? Many agencies take the view that volunteers should be prepared to serve where they are needed, their own choice of country being of secondary importance. How do you feel about this? If you have a specific preference then you should state this when applying, giving your reasons. Questions you should ask yourself about the proposed host country include its location, climate, history and current political situation:

- [ ] Where in the world *is* the country?

- [ ] Could I cope with the heat, the dust, the mosquitoes, the lack of basic facilities?

- [ ] Could I come to terms with the practices and customs of the local host community?

- [ ] Are the priorities of the government of the country the same as those of the majority of the people?

- [ ] If not, why not, and what as a volunteer can I or will I, do?

Terms and conditions As far as terms and conditions of work are concerned, many agencies provide accommodation, board, travel, remuneration and insurance; further details about this are given in each entry or are available from the agencies on application. Some agencies also provide allowances covering equipment, settlement/resettlement, dependants and holidays. You should ascertain how you are to be paid, and by whom, how social security and pension rights are affected and what sort of insurance provision is available. Find out about job security - you may find yourself doing a completely different job from the one you expected, or no work at all, and you will need to know whom you can turn to in such an event. The political and social climate in some countries is not always stable, so find out what security provisions and support you can count on in case of political or social conflict. And what will be your position if, in exceptional circumstances, you return before the end of the contract period?

Projects You should do your best to find out as much as you can about the project to which you will be assigned, bearing in mind the points made in the *Motivation* section about the need for projects to be actually required by the people for whom they are set up. Some agencies recruit volunteers on behalf of organisations overseas and so will not themselves be in control of the project volunteers will be working on, but you should still endeavour to find out the answers to key questions such as:

- [ ] Why was the project chosen?

- [ ] How does it relate to local needs?

- [ ] Who set it up?

- [ ] Who finances it?

- [ ] What do the duties entail?

- [ ] Who would you report to?

- [ ] How are the decisions reached?

- [ ] Why does the project need the skills of a volunteer?

- [ ] Whose interests will your presence promote?

- [ ] How interested is the recruiting agency in the work you will be doing?

If the project is well-established you should be able to see the field reports, evaluations and debriefing records of previous volunteers. If the project is successful, you could ask why the agency has not by now trained a local person to fill the post, and in any case, you should check carefully that by going there you are not putting a local person out of a job.

The publishers are grateful to VSO
for permission to use their photographs throughout this guide

We are also grateful to the United Nations Association International Service,
Independent Living Schemes, Returned Volunteer Action and L'Arche
for allowing us to use first hand accounts from their volunteers

SECTION II

UNDERSTANDING
DEVELOPMENT

INFORMATION
RESOURCES

UNDERSTANDING DEVELOPMENT

There is a certain amount of controversy about the extent to which the industrialised nations are responsible for the under-development of the Third World and what steps should be taken to effect a change in the relationship. If you are considering volunteering as a development worker overseas you should make every effort to find out more about the issues involved and how they affect the situation in the country in which you will be working. If you have recently returned from a period of voluntary work overseas you may be keen to work in the field of development education and awareness-raising.

The following organisations, based in Britain, campaign on a variety of development and environmental issues and/or produce reading materials and other resources of interest to potential and returned volunteers. Note that none of them actually sends volunteers overseas, but many of them do recruit volunteers to help with administration, fundraising, campaigning or publicity in the UK; or there may be a local group, part of a campaigning network involving volunteers.

AMNESTY INTERNATIONAL BRITISH SECTION 99-119 Rosebery Avenue, London EC1R 4RE ✆ 071-814 6200
A voluntarily financed worldwide human rights movement which is independent of any government, political faction, ideology, economic interest or religious creed. It works for the release of prisoners of conscience provided they have never used or advocated violence, advocates fair and early trials for all political prisoners, and opposes the death penalty and torture or other cruel, inhuman or degrading treatment, of all prisoners without reservation. Annual *Amnesty International Report* details its work and main concerns in more than 120 countries and has a factual country-by-country account of human rights abuses; also *Country Reports* and *Theme Reports*. Local groups campaigning network.

APPROPRIATE HEALTH RESOURCES AND TECHNOLOGIES ACTION GROUP (AHRTAG) 1 London Bridge Street, London SE1 9SG ✆ 071-378 1403
A charity which aims to promote primary health care in developing countries and to encourage the development of appropriate

health technologies offering alternatives to high cost medical practice. Library and resource centre available to health workers going to work in developing countries; contains a wide range of relevant books, journals, documents, regularly updated bibliographies and training information. *Publications List* includes newsletters, resource lists, briefing packs and directories covering primary health care.

CAFOD Romero Close, Stockwell Road, London SW9 9TY ✆ 071-733 7900
The official Catholic Church agency in England and Wales for overseas development, aiming to increase awareness of poverty and injustice in the world and the structures which cause them. Promotes human development and social justice in witness to Christian faith and Gospel values, through authentic and practical partnership between communities in the Third World and people in England and Wales. Provides emergency relief and supports over 700 projects in community development, vocational training, preventive health care, food production, water development and non-formal education in some 75 Third World countries. Also runs fundraising and awareness-raising in England and Wales for which voluntary clerical and administrative support is often needed. *Resources Catalogue* lists general books and materials; simulation games; country profiles; and campaigning, theological, social, teaching and liturgical material.

COMMONWEALTH INSTITUTE Kensington High Street, London W8 6NQ ✆ 071-603 4535
The centre for Commonwealth education and culture in Britain. It aims to promote knowledge and understanding of the Commonwealth through a programme of permanent and special exhibitions, cultural events and festivals, and educational activities. Its Commonwealth Resource Centre has multi-media resources and a reference collection providing general factual information about the individual countries, peoples and organisations making up the Commonwealth.

COUNCIL FOR EDUCATION IN WORLD CITIZENSHIP Seymour Mews House, Seymour Mews, London W1H 9PE ✆ 071-935 1752 Fax 071-935 4741
A non-political and non-sectarian organisation promoting such studies, teachings and activities as may best contribute to mutual understanding, peace and cooperation, and goodwill between all peoples. Regular *Broadsheets* provide background information on countries and issues in the news; each has an accompanying *Digest* for younger students and an associated *Activities Sheet*. Bi-monthly *Newsletters* publicise opportunities for young people and their teachers and include new resources for improving education for international understanding selected from more than 200 organisations. CEWC also supports a range of local, regional and national workshops and conferences for young people and their teachers, and its *World Dimensions in the National Curriculum* identifies, for each subject and cross-curricular theme, where the knowledge, skills and understanding relating to international citizenship occur. There is also a Resource Centre and a Speakers Service. Membership is open to individuals, schools, colleges, organisations and local authorities. CEWC receives grants from the UK education departments and others. There are opportunities for volunteers in CEWC's London office (for library, resources, educational, accounting, administrative and clerical work) and, especially for former teachers, with its regional groups all over the

UK, to help organise local workshops and conferences.

FAIRSHARES CONSORTIUM PO Box 23, Marlborough, Wiltshire SN8 1EX

Promotes education and fundraising in relation to the ideal of sustainable development in the Third World. Runs a schools programme and provides speakers.

FRIENDS OF THE EARTH
26-28 Underwood Street, London N1 7JQ
ℂ 071-490 1555

A network of independent national groups in 47 countries, with an International Secretariat based in Amsterdam. In the UK, Friends of the Earth represents the environmental concerns of many thousands of people, blowing the whistle on those who destroy the environment, and putting pressure on those who have the power to protect it. It has over 300 local groups across the UK and more than 80 Earth Action groups for those aged 14-21, campaigning against the destruction of the environment and providing information about environmental issues and ways in which individuals can help save the natural world.

GREENPEACE Canonbury Villas, London N1 2PN ℂ 071-354 5100

An international environmental pressure group which actively campaigns for a nuclear-free future, to stop pollution of the natural world and to protect wildlife. Greenpeace campaigns have one common purpose: to preserve or recreate an environment in which living things, including people, can survive without threat to their lives and health. Campaigns involve non-violent direct action and the lobbying of relevant authorities and international conventions, backed up by scientific studies and careful research. Local Support Groups countrywide organise fundraising initiatives

and occasionally help with lobbying and campaigning. Volunteers are also needed in the London office, where, unless they have particular skills/interests they are usually placed in the Public Information Unit, giving them a chance to learn about Greenpeace and the various campaigns it is working on.

INTERMEDIATE TECHNOLOGY DEVELOPMENT GROUP Myson House, Railway Terrace, Rugby CV21 3HT
ℂ Rugby (0788) 560631

Founded by the late Dr E F Schumacher in the 1960s, IT aims to enable poor people in the Third World to develop and use productive technologies and methods which give them greater control over their own lives and which contribute to the long-term development of their communities. *Publications Catalogue* covers a wide range of books on appropriate technology and development issues, including titles on agriculture, building and construction, cooperatives, education and training, energy sources, health, manufacturing, handicrafts, industry and business, roads and transport, water and sanitation. *Appropriate Technology* quarterly magazine provides reports from the field for those interested in development practice. All publications and subscriptions enquiries to IT Publications, 103-105 Southampton Row, London WC1B 4HH.

INTERNATIONAL BROADCASTING TRUST 2 Ferdinand Place, London NW1 8EE
ℂ 071-482 2847

Promotes public awareness about world development through the production of television and radio programmes for broadcast in the UK and overseas. Publishes educational materials to accompany the programmes, and promotes the use of the programmes and publications in schools and adult education. Short-term volunteers are often needed in researching and planning programmes, and in administrative work.

THE LATIN AMERICA BUREAU 1 Amwell Street, London EC1R 1UL ✆ 071-278 2829
A small, independent, non-profitmaking research organisation established in 1977, concerned with human rights and related social, political and economic issues in Central and South America and the Caribbean. Carries out research, publishes books and establishes support links with Latin American groups. Library has a collection of periodicals from and about the region. Acts as subscription agent for the magazine *Report on the Americas* published five times a year by the New York based North American Congress on Latin America (NACLA). *Books Catalogue* includes publications, resources for education, studies in Latin American culture and country guides.

MINORITY RIGHTS GROUP 379 Brixton Road, London SW9 7DE ✆ 071-978 9498
An international human rights organisation investigating a whole range of minority and majority situations in the world arising from discrimination and prejudice. Works through the UN and other international bodies to increase awareness of human rights issues, and fosters international understanding of the factors which create prejudiced treatment and group tensions, helping to promote the growth of a world conscience regarding human rights. Has 69 *Reports* on the problems of a wide range of oppressed groups in Africa, the Americas, Asia, Southern Oceans, Middle East and Europe.

OVERSEAS DEVELOPMENT INSTITUTE Regent's College, Inner Circle, Regent's Park, London NW1 4NS ✆ 071-487 7413
Founded in 1960 as an independent non-governmental centre for development

research and a forum for discussion of the problems facing developing countries. Produces regular *Briefing Papers* which analyse contemporary development issues, available free. *Publications List* includes books, working papers, occasional papers, reports and journals covering a range of subjects including finance and economics, trade and industry, development policy, environmental economics, agricultural development and disasters. The ODI Library, a specialist collection of approx 20,000 books and 400 periodical titles covering a variety of development issues is open to visitors from 09.30-17.30, Tuesdays - Thursdays.

OXFAM 274 Banbury Road, Oxford OX2 7DZ ✆ Oxford (0865) 311311 (switchboard) or 312306 (volunteers)
Oxfam works with poor people regardless of race or religion in their struggle against hunger, disease, exploitation and poverty in Africa, Asia, Latin America and the Caribbean and the Middle East, through relief, development, research overseas, and public education at home. Oxfam is first and foremost a development agency and, although it still provides relief in times of crisis, its main concern is long-term sustainable development. Oxfam does not recruit volunteers to work overseas but volunteers are needed to work at the headquarters in Oxford, 12 regional offices, and over 900 shops throughout Britain. Unpaid education workers are also needed to visit schools, and there are local groups countrywide involved in campaigning. Publications, newsletters and other resource materials are distributed for sale as part of Oxfam's education, campaigning and information programme, and cover a variety of countries and topics including trade, environment, land and food, development practice, training, gender and health, as well as reference guides, maps and

activity packs. *Development in Practice* journal published three times a year provides a forum for the exchange of ideas and information among policy makers and staff both North and South, and carries articles and assessments of the experiences of Oxfam and other NGOs. All publications and subscriptions enquiries to Oxfam Publications, PO Box 120, Oxford OX2 7FA ✆ Oxford (0865) 312415.

POPULATION CONCERN 231 Tottenham Court Road, London W1P 9AE ✆ 071-6379582
Raises funds for overseas population and development programmes. Campaigns on population and related issues in the education field and amongst the general public. There are opportunties for short-term volunteers to work in its information service and on fundraising, education and sometimes project work.

SURVIVAL INTERNATIONAL 310 Edgware Road, London W2 1DY ✆ 071-723 5535
A worldwide movement to support tribal peoples, standing for their right to decide their own future and helping them protect their lands, environment and way of life. Stocks a wide selection of books, reports and other documentation on tribal peoples and the issues affecting them, and produces a bi-annual *Survival Newsletter*. Audio and visual materials, including slide sets, video tapes and photo exhibitions are also available for sale or hire. Volunteers are needed to work on a variety of tasks in the London office.

THIRD WORLD FIRST 217 Cowley Road, Oxford OX4 1XG ✆ Oxford (0865) 245678/ 723832 Fax (0865) 200179
A national movement in colleges and universities, explaining and campaigning against the causes of poverty, hunger and

exploitation in the Third World, and supporting the growing efforts of the poor as they organise together to determine their own development. *Publications List* covers books, magazines and fact sheets on world development issues including health, women, aid, disarmament, racism, environment and debt.

TOOLS FOR SELF RELIANCE Netley Marsh Workshops, Netley Marsh, Southampton SO4 2GY ✆ (0703) 869697
Founded to increase the self reliance of villages in the Third World by providing handtools. A network of local groups collect unwanted handtools, which are refurbished and sent to Third World communities. Also promotes an awareness of bonds with the Third World to establish a more fair and just society.

UK COMMITTEE FOR UNICEF 55 Lincoln's Inn Fields, London WC2A 3NB ✆ 071-405 5592
UNICEF is an integral but semi-autonomous part of the United Nations, addressing the problems of children in the developing world, serving 128 countries and working in social services, nutrition, emergency relief and rehabilitation, water/sanitation, primary health care and formal/non-formal education. *The State of the World's Children* reports on the progress of strategies for child survival, and the simple and low-cost methods that could bring about a dramatic improvement in the well-being of the world's children. Produces books, information packs and study materials.

WAR ON WANT Fenner Brockway House, 37-39 Great Guildford Street, London SE1 0ES ✆ 071-620 1111
International aid agency actively campaigning against injustice and oppression in developing countries and for increasing

awareness in the UK of the causes of world poverty. Funds long-term and emergency relief in famine areas torn by military struggle, where little international aid is sent. Network of local groups in Britain where those interested can find out more about the issues and help with fundraising.

Also recruits volunteers for administrative work in London office. *Resources* list covers leaflets, information packs and publications concerned with health, childcare, women, famine, development issues, politics, exploitation and oppression.

WATERAID 1 Queen Anne's Gate, London SW1H 9BT ✆ 071-222 8111

Concerned with long-term development rather than emergency relief, WaterAid provides Third World communities, through personnel training and organisation, with the materials and technical backup needed to improve drinking water supply, sanitation and associated health education. Material support is given to several indigenous Third World organisations through a UK network of voluntary engineering advisors.

WORLD DEVELOPMENT MOVEMENT 25 Beehive Place, London SW9 7QR ✆ 071-737 6215

A democratic, non party political organisation existing solely to campaign for political changes to tackle the causes of world poverty. Campaigns cover issues such as debt relief, fair trade, environmentally sensitive development and other economic policies. WDM has a nationwide network linking individual members, local action groups, lobby teams and support staff. Members receive *Spur* newspaper six times a year which gives campaign news and information, notices of urgent action, and details of links with other WDM groups.

WORLDAWARE Centre for World Development Education, 1 Catton Street, London WC1R 4AB ✆ 071-831 3844

An independent agency whose main aim is to promote education in Britain about world development issues and Britain's interdependence with the Third World; funded partly by the Overseas Development Administration. Annual *Catalogue* includes a wide range of handbooks, guides, booklets, information sheets and other materials on world development and interdependence; employment, technology, industry and energy; EC and the Third World; aid; disasters and refugees; immigrants and migration; population and education; and health, food and agriculture.

INFORMATION   RESOURCES

The information provided on each volunteer-sending agency or advisory body includes details of relevant briefing and other information resources. This list provides further reading material, including additional volunteer placement opportunities and background material on volunteering and development issues.

VOLUNTARY WORK

The Voluntary Agencies Directory £10.95 is a comprehensive listing of voluntary agencies in the UK, compiled by the National Council for Voluntary Organisations. It lists nearly 2000 agencies ranging from small, specialist self-help groups to established national charities. An invaluable source of reference for anyone thinking about doing volunteer work in the UK. Published by NCVO Publications, Regent's Wharf, 8 All Saints Street, London N1 9RL ✆ 071-713 6161.

The Working Overseas Resource Pack £6 including postage is a selection of booklets about volunteering and development, published by Returned Volunteer Action. Includes information about the main sending agencies and their volunteer requirements, a summary of the role of volunteering in the development process, and a discussion of how development education in parallel with overseas work can help towards long-term change. There are also details of RVA's information and training events, local contacts and returned volunteer database. Available from RVA, 1 Amwell Street, London EC1R 1UL ✆ 071-278 0804.

The HPA Guide to Voluntary Nursing Overseas £2.50 including postage, provides information on the many organisations which send nurses abroad, as well as general information on working overseas. Available from Health Projects Abroad, HMS President (1918), Victoria Embankment, London EC4Y 0HJ ✆ 071-583 5725.

Working Holidays £8.95 is an annual guide to thousands of seasonal work opportunities in

Britain and around the world. Gives details of a wide variety of short-term voluntary placements, including workcamps, community work, archaeological digs, conservation and restoration projects. There is also helpful practical advice on travel, insurance, accommodation and further sources of information. Published by the Central Bureau for Educational Visits and Exchanges, Seymour Mews House, Seymour Mews, London W1H 9PE ✆ 071-486 5101.

Jobs Abroad is a directory of over 3000 opportunities of interest to Christians, published twice a year price £1.20 plus 65p postage.
STS Directory is a yearly manual of short-term Christian service opportunities in the UK and abroad, price £1.20 plus 65p postage.
Who Needs You? gives information on opportunities for voluntary Christian service for those working from home, price 30p plus an A5 SAE.
All available from the Christian Service Centre, Holloway Street West, Lower Gornal, Dudley, West Midlands DY3 2DZ ✆ Dudley (0902) 882836.

A Place for you Overseas is a series of leaflets, price 10p each, giving information on openings through many organisations and schemes.
Opportunities Abroad is a six-monthly list of current vacancies through about 40 volunteer mission agencies, price £1.
A Place for you in Britain leaflets, price 10p each, cover openings in the UK as a volunteer.
All available from Christians Abroad, 1 Stockwell Green, London SW9 9HP (add 30p to cover postage).

Invest Yourself: The Catalogue of Volunteer Opportunities is a comprehensive guide to short to long-term volunteer opportunities

with North American non-profit organisations, both in North America and worldwide. Published by the Commission on Voluntary Service & Action, PO Box 117-37X, New York, United States, price US$10.

International Directory of Voluntary Work £8.95 is a guide to short and long-term volunteer opportunities in Britain and abroad.
The Directory of Work and Study in Developing Countries £7.95 is a guide to employment, voluntary work, and academic opportunities in the Third World.
Both published by Vacation Work, 9 Park End Street, Oxford OX1 1HJ ✆ Oxford (0865) 241978.

Volunteer! The Comprehensive Guide to Voluntary Service in the US and Abroad $8.95 plus $7 airmail postage, lists over 200 voluntary service organisations offering voluntary opportunities ranging in length from a few days to a few years. Published by the Council for International Educational Exchange and the Council of Religious Volunteer Agencies, and available from CIEE, Publications Department, 205 East 42nd Street, New York, NY 10017, United States.

Workcamp Organisers lists nearly 280 national and international voluntary service organisations sponsoring workcamps in approx 90 countries. It includes the duration of the camps, months in which they take place, type of work, financial conditions and other details. Published every 3 years in cooperation with the Youth Division of UNESCO by the Coordinating Committee for International Voluntary Service, UNESCO, 1 rue Miollis, 75015 Paris, France. Cost FF12 or 14 IRCs.

The Canadian Guide to Working and Living Overseas is a complete reference guide for anyone thinking of undertaking paid or voluntary work in another country. Profiles hundreds of organisations and employers and offers invaluable advice from job-hunting to overcoming expatriate isolation. Published by Intercultural Systems, PO Box 588, Station B, Ottawa, Ontarion, Canada K1P 5P7, price Can$34.50.

DEVELOPMENT ISSUES

Earthscan Publications Ltd, 120 Pentonville Road, London N1 9JN © 071-278 0433 is an editorially independent subsidiary of Kogan Page Ltd, publishing in association with the International Institute for Environment and Development and the World Wide Fund for Nature (UK). Its *Catalogue* covers a wide range of books on environmental and development issues.

IT Publications, 103-105 Southampton Row, London WC1B 4HH is the publications wing of the Intermediate Technology Development Group. Its *Publications Catalogue* includes books on appropriate technology and development issues, including titles on agriculture, building and construction, cooperatives, education and training, energy sources, health, manufacturing, handicrafts, industry and business, roads and transport, water and sanitation.
Appropriate Technology quarterly magazine provides reports from the field for those interested in development practice.

New Internationalist, 55 Rectory Road, Oxford OX4 1BW © Oxford (0865) 728181 is a monthly magazine covering major world issues. Produced by a cooperative based in Oxford and with offices in Aotearoa/New Zealand, Australia and Canada. Originally started in 1973 with the backing of major aid agencies such as Oxfam, but is now

independent with over 70,000 subscribers worldwide. Each month the magazine covers a different Third World/Environmental theme, such as global warming, Southern Africa or animal rights, with plenty of analysis, facts, opinions, photographs and charts.

Oxfam Publications, PO Box 120, Oxford OX2 7FA © Oxford (0865) 312415 cover a variety of countries and topics including trade, environment, land and food, development practice, training, gender and health, as well as reference guides, maps and activity packs. *Development in Practice* journal published three times a year provides a forum for the exchange of ideas and information among policy makers and staff both North and South, and carries articles and assessments of the experiences of Oxfam and other NGOs.

Zed Books, 57 Caledonian Road, London N1 9BU © 071-837 8466 publish titles covering a wide range of development issues and areas including Third World Women, Development and the Environment, Women and World Development, Health, the Middle East, Africa and Asia.

United Nations Development Education Directory details the work of each United Nations agency in the field of development education. Available from United Nations Non-Governmental Liaison Service, Palais des Nations, 1211 Geneva 10, Switzerland.

Development Forum is a bi-monthly newspaper covering all development issues and the work of organisations, from local grassroots to international perspectives. Available on annual subscription from United Nations Department of Public Information, PO Box 5850, Grand Central Station, New York, United States.

Further details on publications and other resources covering development and related issues are given under the individual entries of the organisations listed in the *Understanding Development* section.

TAKING A YEAR OUT

A Year Between £8.99 is a complete guide for those taking a year out between school and higher education or work, or higher education and a career. Carefully researched with the aspirations of school leavers and graduates in mind, it offers authoritative advice and guidance, as well as relating the experiences of people who have themselves taken a year out. Published by the Central Bureau for Educational Visits and Exchanges, Seymour Mews House, Seymour Mews, London W1H 9PE ✆ 071-486 5101.

Opportunities in the Gap Year £3 looks at what is available to sixth-formers wishing to take a break between school and university or college. It weighs up the pros and cons of a year out and gives hints on how to make the best of a once-in-a-lifetime opportunity. Published by the Independent Schools Careers Organisation, 12a-18a Princess Way, Camberley, Surrey GU15 3SP ✆ Camberley (0276) 21188.

Taking a Year Off £7.95 takes a new look at the option of taking time out before, during or after higher education or during employment, encouraging the reader to identify his or her own needs by placing emphasis on case studies, group discussions and interviews, letters, a quiz, checklists, and the experiences of young people who have taken time out. Published by Trotman and Company Limited, 12-14 Hill Rise, Richmond, Surrey TW10 6UA.

TRAVEL

Sources of Information for Independent and Overland Travellers £3 is a reference guide giving details on where to get the best information about health, equipment, visas, insurance, maps and so on. Published by the Expedition Advisory Centre of the Royal Geographical Society, 1 Kensington Gore, London SW7 2AR ✆ 071-581 2057.

The Travellers' Handbook £11.95 (£6.95 to members) is an 852 page reference and source book for the independent traveller, with chapters on travel, camping and backpacking, hitch-hiking, health, clothing, luggage and survival kits, where to stay, dealing with people when things go wrong, photography, choosing maps, passports, visas, permits, insurance, currency and Customs. Also includes special chapters for students, single women and people with a disability. Published by WEXAS International, 45-49 Brompton Road, London SW3 1DE ✆ 071-589 0500.

The Tropical Traveller by John Hatt is an invaluable handbook for those travelling to and through tropical countries. Published by Penguin, and available in most good bookshops, price £7.99.

Lonely Planet's *Travel Survival Kits* and *Shoestring* guides are detailed handbooks to many countries worldwide, giving background information on the country, advice on places to visit, information on where to stay, what to eat, how to get there and ways to travel around. Also produce a rang of useful *Phrasebooks* containing essential words and phrases for effective communication with local people. Available in most good bookshops; prices range from £1.95 for some of the smaller phrasebooks through to £14.95 for the bigger travel guides.

Rough Guides are a series of practical handbooks to most countries in Europe and some areas of Asia, South America and the United States, giving full details on cities, towns and places of interest, plus a wealth of practical information on places to stay and how to get around. The range also includes *Women Travel*, a guide for women travellers; also *Nothing Ventured: disabled people travel the world* containing first-hand accounts of disabled people's travel experiences and practical advice on planning a trip. Published by Penguin and available in most good bookshops; prices range from £6.99-£11.99.

Culture Shock! is a series of cultural guides written for international travellers of any background. The reader is introduced to the people, customs, ceremonies, food and culture of a country, with checklists of dos and don'ts. Countries currently in the series include Australia, Britain, Canada, China, France, India, Indonesia, Israel, Italy, Japan, Korea, Malaysia, Nepal, Pakistan, the Philippines, Singapore, Sri Lanka, Thailand and the USA. All guides cost £6.95 and are available from bookshops or through Kuperard (London) Ltd, No 9, Hampstead West, 224 Iverson Road, West Hampstead, London NW6 2HL ✆ 071-372 4722.

PREPARATION & TRAINING

Some preparation is obviously needed, and it is in the volunteer's interest to inform themselves about the country they will be living and working in, as well as to request adequate training from the agency before setting out. Any agency with a sense of responsibility will make available time and find funds for proper training, and such an orientation period should last long enough for you to both take in and digest the information.

You may be about to live and work in a society where much will be strange and different, and the training is basically to help you understand and cope. There should be a chance to discuss development and other issues of concern to the host country, as well as arrangements for you to meet other volunteers, both those who are about to leave and those who have recently returned. A knowledge of the relevant language is also vital in enabling you to make contact with ordinary people. Even in countries where English is an official language only a small proportion of the population may speak it (often a privileged minority) so the agency should provide at least basic language instruction. You should also receive up-to-date and relevant technical advice relating to your sphere of work, and any special technologies that fit within the context of development.

In some cases more emphasis is placed on training within the host country, and, depending on the agency, you may on arrival spend anything from a few days to a few months on an orientation programme, acclimatising yourself, learning the language, finding out about the culture and people and the type of work you will be doing. Training should also be a continuing process carried on at intervals throughout the period of service, allowing volunteers to update their skills and make regular reports about their project, and including some preparation for the return home.

There is usually more than enough time before placement and actual departure to allow personal preparation and information gathering to be undertaken. In addition to acquiring a knowledge of the future host country/area through analysis of its socio-economic background, politics, history, culture and living conditions, try to assimilate some popular aspects through food, crafts, arts and music. It is often possible to meet with some nationals of that country, for example higher education students studying in your own country.

Involve your family and friends as much as possible. This will help when the trauma of the departure day itself actually arrives, and will help in maintaining contact throughout your placement. Training should be seen as an opportunity not only to be briefed for the work you will be undertaking, but also to prepare for many of the events and eventualities you will face.

In this way, the inevitable stress brought on by months of anticipation, the change in home, in cultural environment, in the work environment if not in the job itself, and in friends, will to some extent be cushioned. If the shock of a new culture, to be experienced on many levels, is seen as a positive element of the whole process of placement, then the rewards will be gained earlier and less painfully. Being immersed in an environment and community radically different from one's own can have a variety of effects, and at different stages of the project.

The initial feeling on arrival at the placement, often after a lengthy period of preparation, may be simply one of euphoria, where cultural and other differences may be brushed aside as you come to terms with the reality of months of anticipation. Much may be viewed in a too positive light, the *manyana* attitudes of co-workers seen as relaxing, not inefficient, the overwhelming friendliness as a natural

welcome, not overfamiliarity. You are not isolated in your new surroundings, as you may have imagined, but are overwhelmed. Before long however, you will need to build yourself a new social structure. Without some established order, minor difficulties may take on the form of major disasters. Remember that your personal state will very much affect the success, or otherwise, of the project. This stage of adjustment will be similar to that gone through with any new job, where tension and anxiety can quickly build up as you strive to prove yourself while at the same time coming to terms with great changes on many fronts. On a voluntary placement in another country, these tensions may be compounded by language, indifferent health in foreign surroundings, utter loneliness, and an inability to adapt quickly enough.

How long this culture fatigue lasts will depend on you, the thoroughness of your preparation, the support from the placing agency, the length of the project itself, and above all your tolerance. It is no accident that many volunteer-sending agencies put a sense of humour fairly high on the agenda of required qualities. The ability to laugh, particularly at yourself, will see you through many a dip as goals seem ever unachievable, as success appears distant, and as homesickness or boredom threatens to overwhelm.

One particular problem will be to separate your private life and your work life. Your personal skills may be as much in demand on the placement as your professional skills. The size and form of your host community may make any sort of privacy almost impossible. Much however, will depend on the nature of the task in hand, how *you* view the challenges ahead, and above all, how prepared you really are for a new work and life style.

Further information about specific countries and development issues can be obtained from the organisations listed in the *Understanding Development* section. The following agencies also arrange specialist briefing courses for those about to go overseas:

ACTION HEALTH 2000 The Gate House, 25 Gwydir Street, Cambridge CB1 2LG ℂ/Fax Cambridge (0223) 460853

An international voluntary health association working for better health care in parts of Asia and East Africa by creating greater awareness of the issues involved and giving practical support to appropriate health programmes. Organises a weekend orientation course for health personnel and development workers planning to work overseas, covering health and development, country briefings, personal health care and survival, travel, insurance, fundraising and communication skills. Opportunity to meet and talk with those who have worked in developing countries.

THE CENTRE FOR INTERNATIONAL BRIEFING Farnham Castle, Farnham, Surrey GU9 0AG ℂ Farnham (0252) 721194

A non-profit educational organisation providing 4-day residential briefing courses for those, including volunteers, who have been appointed to work in the developing countries of Africa, Latin America and the Caribbean, Asia and the Pacific, and the Middle East. The courses provide an understanding of the working environment and cover the culture, values and attitudes, history, the political, social and economic structure, current affairs, future trends and living conditions of the destination country. Intensive language tuition is available throughout the year for most languages. Also arrange courses on Britain for those from overseas who have recently arrived to take up residence, especially on professional development assignments.

THE CHRISTIAN SERVICE CENTRE Holloway Street West, Lower Gornal, Dudley, West Midlands DY3 2DZ

Member of the Evangelical Missionary Alliance and the Evangelical Alliance, offering information and advice to those interesting in doing long-term Christian Service. Organises regular *Which Way?* weekends and days for those seriously considering where God wants them. Subjects include world mission, guidance, training for service, opportunities available and personal evaluation. For further details and a booking form write enclosing SAE.

Also publish directories listing opportunities for short and long-term Christian service in Britain and overseas.

CHRISTIANS ABROAD 1 Stockwell Green, London SW9 9HP ℂ 071-737 7811

An ecumenical body, supported by aid and mission agencies, with over 20 years' experience of vocational guidance for those seeking overseas opportunities.

Arranges *New Eyes* half-day workshops for groups interested in exploring the possibility of working overseas. Staff work with groups of 10 or more to enable group members to look objectively at their skills, experience and circumstances; present a range of opportunities for overseas work; provide tools for decision-,making and explore ways of preparing to apply to work overseas. Sessions include a skills audit; how an individual's circumstances may affect openings; a discussion of available options; decisions; and developing a portfolio.

RETURNED VOLUNTEER ACTION
1 Amwell Street, London EC1R 1UL
✆ 071-278 0804
An organisation of, and for, serving and
returned volunteers, those interested in or
active in development work, and others who
worked overseas. Organises *Questioning
Development Days* every few months for
prospective volunteers, where they can talk to
returned volunteers in informal discussion
sessions. Can also put prospective volunteers
in touch with others who have done similar
work or volunteered in the same country.
Publishes a range of titles including a *Working
Overseas* resource pack containing information
on sending agencies and general information
for the prospective overseas worker/
volunteer; *Questioning Development; Handbook
for Development Workers Overseas; Thinking
About Volunteering; Volunteers in Health Care:
Food for Thought;* and *For Whose Benefit?*

THE VOLUNTEER MISSIONARY
MOVEMENT Comboni House, London
Road, Sunningdale, Ascot, Berkshire SL5 0JY
✆ Ascot (0344) 875380
An ecumenical movement within the Catholic
Church which recruits, prepares and sends
Christian volunteers with a skill or profession
to work as lay missionaries in projects linked
with local churches. Organises and runs a
5-week residential preparation course to help
those who are going overseas to reflect upon
and examine their motivation, and to provide
them with relevant up-to-date information.
The course covers all aspects of life and work
overseas and participants learn about the
people with whom they will be working and
the countries and projects in which they will
work. Underlying the course is the missionary element, with special emphasis placed on
prayer, spiritual formation and guidance,
with returned volunteers sharing their
experiences.

V O I C E S   O F   E X P E R I E N C E

In the sections of practical information and advice there are accounts from volunteers and sending agencies alike, to give some idea of the realities of voluntary service. Here we have included some personal insights into what it actually means to give and to receive.

Many project placements are unique and every volunteer different, and each will have their own idea of what it is they have personally gained from volunteering. Nonetheless it is always worth getting some first-hand information before you start any project. A friend who has been a volunteer may be able to give you some advice and information, and the organisation you will be working for should be happy to provide you with a list of returned volunteers whom you can contact.

Sarah Lane answered a UNAIS advert for a speech/language therapist to work in Sucre, Bolivia. Over a year later, after completing a six month course in Cochabamba learning Spanish and about life in Bolivia, she finally arrived in Sucre. Here she shares her first impressions of the place where she will be living and working for the next two years:

Sucre was as beautiful as everyone had told me, full of colonial buildings, freshly painted and dazzling white. It's a small city, surrounded by mountains, so that when you look along a street you can see where the city ends and the hills start.

I have a wonderful view from my window at work, no comparison at all to the brick wall I used to see from my office in Camberwell!

I've been here three weeks now, and the city is small enough so that when you walk around town you are very likely to bump into someone you know, which gives a nice feeling of belonging here - though of course I don't know anyone well yet.

My first encounter with Hermano Maximiliano, who runs the Centro Psicopedagogica, a centre for children with learning difficulties and physical handicaps, was interesting. He was, of course, nothing like my stereotyped idea of a monk, added to which he speaks Spanish very quickly with a strong Spanish accent, so I had great difficulty understanding him.

How can I possibly be a Spanish language therapist when I don't speak the language well? How will anyone have any confidence in my ability to do this job? However, my first impressions of the Centre were very positive - everyone seemed very welcoming and demonstrated a warm and caring attitude towards the children.

It's a time of change here, and therefore a good time for me to be starting. However, it has been two years since the Centre first requested a speech/language therapist, and I have a feeling they are expecting miracles!

I am trying to lower expectations a little, and am also talking about different aspects of language and communication, not just speech, but the understanding of language too.

I'm the only speech/language therapist in Sucre; there are a few elsewhere in Bolivia; but all have been trained abroad as there is no training available here yet. There is obviously a great need for such training, however; I keep meeting people who know someone who has some kind of communication difficulty. My job will involve working with out-patients as well as children at the Centre.

My first couple of weeks at work have been spent getting to know people, and thinking about the best way of using my time here over the next two years. Training will be an important part of my work, so that when I leave the teachers will be able to continue working with the children to facilitate their language development. Regular training sessions have already been arranged for 8 am every Monday morning!

I have ambitious plans for producing a manual which teachers can use to assess the children's language abilities, together with some ideas for suitable activities to stimulate language development and communicative ability.

I'm still working out the best way to approach things, though - where to start, what to do first and who does what. Roles are slightly different here; for example the physiotherapists work very much under the direction of one of the doctors, and make few decisions themselves. Also, the scarcity of resources is a major factor, even more so than in the NHS.

For example, there are no small wheelchairs; the few wheelchairs there are are too big for the small children who need them, so consequently a few children spend most of their time lying on mattresses looking at the ceiling - which is hardly stimulating!

Although at times I feel fairly daunted by the task ahead, I feel excited about the opportunity to work at the Centre, and potentially to make a difference to the lives of some of the children there, both now and in the future (at least that's the theory).

And I also feel lucky to be living in such a beautiful place, and in such an interesting country.

I'm still getting used to speaking Spanish all the time - on the whole it's not too difficult with the children, but problems arise when I want to explain something to teachers and parents. I often find myself saying something that only approximates to what I want to say.

The last three weeks here have rushed by. I haven't had time to do any of the touristy things like visiting the cathedral ... well, I've got two years here, I'm sure I'll manage it sometime!

Maintenance officer Andrew Dutton is on placement with VSO, restoring neglected school facilities in Papua New Guinea:

The water's off again, mister has got to be the phrase I've heard more than any other since arriving at my new posting in Papua New Guinea. I'm a maintenance officer at Kupiano Provincial High School, situated in Central Province, three hours south-east of the capital, Port Moresby.

Little maintenance has been done since the school opened in the mid-70s, and the conditions the students live and study in are far from satisfactory. This problem extends throughout PNG - Central province alone has eight high schools which need upgrading, but Kupiano is one of the more run-down schools. I'm working within the province's new maintenance programme, along with a manager and a fellow volunteer at a neighbouring school.

When I arrived the students' toilets and washrooms were in such poor condition that the majority couldn't be used. This was due to a combination of neglect, vandalism (on the boys' part) and mainly an erratic water supply. The 150 boy boarders were reduced to washing under a single standpipe and using two badly constructed pit latrines (a student told me that the smaller boys used the floor because they were frightened they might fall down the hole). The girls, who tend to take more care of their facilities, were still using their toilets and wash-rooms, though they were far from perfect.

Over the last two months, Wilson, a young man from the local village, and I have repaired six 9,000-litre water tanks that have been leaking for years, and connected the tanks to provide round-the-clock water.

Upgrading the dormitories will be the next project.

Kupiano is my second posting in PNG - I did a similar job at a school in Milne Bay Province for two years. My time here has been one of the most enjoyable and satisfying periods of my life. It's not always easy, and at times it can be very frustrating, but that all adds to the challenge.

I have found the people here very understanding and accepting of my disability (I lost my right arm in an accident in 1976). My fellow workmen have an uncanny ability to offer help when it's really needed and have no prejudices, which cannot always be said in the UK.

Marek worked as a full time volunteer on an Independent Living Scheme in Lewisham. The job consisted of working alongside a team of two other volunteers, helping a severely disabled man to live an independent life in his own home in the local community:

I found the experience both challenging and rewarding. It proved interesting getting to know the user and other volunteers, plus the other people that were involved more indirectly on the project, all of whom were from a varied background.

Most volunteers stay on the scheme between four and eight months, and after I completed my term I felt a sense of achievement. Before coming to Lewisham I had been unemployed, so I felt I had served a useful purpose on the project and regained much self-confidence. Of course working there was not all a bed of roses. One had to learn to live on a small amount of money, budget oneself, and live alongside and get on with the other volunteers who stayed in the workers' flat. But I felt that all this was a very good learning experience particularly for younger volunteers who were away from home for the first time. Working on an Independent Living Scheme can teach independence and gives an opportunity to get to know a different area away from one's home background. Whatever one's reasons are for becoming a volunteer I am sure everyone gains something from the experience, like I did, through learning a bit about oneself and others. If one has time on hand the ILS Scheme is definitely worth a gamble.

Hazel is a disabled woman whose life has been changed through the Independent Living Scheme:

I never had an independent life before living in the scheme. Up until two years ago I was institutionalised.

The difference is, here you are able to live your own life. You have freedom of choice about the things that most people just take for granted. For example, I mean things like: when I want to get up or go to bed, what to eat, how I want it cooked, what I want to buy ... just the basic things really.

One of the things I really enjoy about it is that we meet so many different people, although I personally get very attached to the people who work with us, so it is hard when they leave. However, if there is someone you have not got on with too well .. at least they don't stay too long!
In residential care, you are living with people who you don't want to be with. You have to do what everyone else does all through the day. If you don't fit in with the

system of the house, you know it's: that one's an awkward case! Staff don't have time to talk things over and the tension builds up. I can now be totally open about everything and, because I've met so many people in my life, I can tell if one of the helpers is upset or worried about anything. We have time now to sit and talk it through.

One thing I'd like to add is that independent living works for a lot of people, but there are a few who need more support than others and for those, maybe four or five of them could share a small group scheme. I would like to see the day when residential care is shut down altogether.

Clare Hall-Matthews has worked as a volunteer in Kent's L'Arche Community for four years. Here she writes about what she has gained from her experience:

I came to L'Arche from an academic background, having completed my degree. I was looking for something different - I wanted to work on relationships, on the heart, after years of educating the head. I certainly found it. Living closely with others, in a caring and open atmosphere, I learned a lot about myself.

I didn't like all of it - I discovered my anger, tension and frustration; I realised there were people I didn't get on with. Sometimes I felt I was pushed to my limits. But still I was accepted and supported. L'Arche has been a place of enormous growth for me.

The way of life seems very normal. We get up and have breakfast, go to work or work in the houses, come home, have supper together, relax in the evenings, go out or go shopping at weekends. But there is a place

for everyone, however handicapped - they
are included and accepted, enabled to join
in.

There is something very simple yet profound
in this. Life is very ordinary, full of
everyday joys and sorrows. We laugh
together, we enjoy each other's company.
We go through difficult times together,
argue, work through problems, share crises.
We learn and grow and pray together.
In L'Arche the assistants are enabling those
with learning difficulties, but it also works
the other way round; the people with
learning disabilities, in sharing with the
assistants, enrich the quality of our lives,
teach us to care, enable us to grow.
The atmosphere of care extends to everyone -
the assistants are supported in their
difficulties and weaknesses too.

People with learning difficulties have a lot
to teach us. Our society values
achievement, success, technology, physical
beauty and prowess. Where does that leave
those who do not succeed? In L'Arche we
learn the unique value of every person,
however handicapped; we learn to appreciate
their gift. When we slow down to their
pace, we gain a new perspective on life and
learn what really matters. We learn to
value relationship and things of the heart.
People are important, not status or success.

When the element of competition is removed
and a place is made for each person, there is
a place for me too. I was able to open up,
and to share my vulnerability. Living with
handicapped people I discovered my own
handicap, my own brokenness. I was also
accepted and loved. I came to L'Arche
with little self-confidence, and although I
still have a long way to go, I gained an
enormous amount.

EXPERIENCE THE CHALLENGE

Volunteering is a creative and proven way of tackling today's social needs, and for 30 years Community Service Volunteers (CSV) has created opportunities for people to play an active part in the life of their community through volunteering, training, education and the media. CSV believes that everyone has got something to give and aims to enable every citizen to invest their energy to help others. Roger Mortlock and Donna Miller here outline the challenges and rewards of community involvement.

Community Service Volunteers challenges all young people to experience the rewards, hard work and fun of working as a volunteer. CSV involves over 2,500 volunteers every year on community projects working face-to-face with people who need their help.

CSV was founded in 1962 with the firm belief that everyone has something to offer the community. It gives everyone the chance to volunteer; no-one is rejected. CSVs may be graduates, school leavers, professionals, homeless, under the care of local authorities, young offenders or substance abusers. The first CSV may have been an Oxbridge candidate, but 30 years on, a CSV is just as likely to be unemployed, disadvantaged or a young offender.

All the volunteers provide an effective and innovative response to current changes in health and social service care; in particular the *1991 Children Act* and the *1990 Community Care Act*. CSVs provide much-needed respite care and support to hard-pressed carers of elderly relatives or family members with disabilities. They help other young people get established when leaving local authority care by teaching them basic skills to live on their own, like cooking, budgeting or looking for employment. In Coventry, CSVs organise other young people to educate their peers about the hazards of unprotected sex and issues surrounding HIV/AIDS.

After 20 years of working with young offender institutions, CSV now recruits full-time volunteers from adult open prisons. Young people can come to CSV for a meaningful activity while on a community sentence or after release from custody. Being a CSV may be the first time a young person has experienced real responsibility and shown that they care for other people. Offenders join other young people from different walks of life and have the chance to break the stereotypes and prove it's the person - and not the offence - that counts.

When she received her Probation Order, Anita's Probation Officer suggested CSV. Working in a home for adults with learning disabilities for six months proved a challenge and a turning point for Anita. She was accepted without question by the people she worked with and found that working in new surroundings helped her to break away from a pattern of offending.

In these and many other settings young CSVs complement the work already being done by professional staff and do not attempt to replace it. The contribution made by CSVs can make the difference between living and just being alive for the people they help.

By the year 2000, more that one third of the UK's population, over 17 million people, will be aged over 50. Improvements in health care and working conditions mean that most people remain healthy and active well into their later years. But once the honeymoon period of retirement has ended and time at home begins to drag, more and more people are deciding to use their skills, time and energy to help others in the community.

CSV's Retired and Senior Volunteer Programme, RSVP, not only helps local communities, it enables older people to stay fit, healthy and active through volunteering. RSVP believes that all volunteers have the knowledge and wisdom to be of immense value to their local community.

Jean Anderson, an RSVP volunteer in Glasgow:

It gives me a purpose in life, I feel if I wasn't doing this I'd need to look for something else to do because I'm on my own now. Why retire and just sit there and vegetate when you can be of use to the community and give?

RSVP is targeting the largest untapped source of voluntary help there is, a reserve of people with time and skills to invest which is continually growing as the UK population grows older. At the same time within every local community and in hard-pressed health and social services, there is a need for the enthusiasm and energy of volunteers - in schools, hospitals, day centres, museums, in protecting the environment and visiting the sick and housebound.

RSVP brings together those organisations who are clamouring for volunteers with older people looking to fill their lives actively and positively. RSVP is pioneering a new approach to volunteering that is entirely volunteer-led.

Many older volunteers are re-investing their skills and experience in schools - sharing memories and living history of World War II, organising carpentry or cookery groups and working with pupils on reading and numeracy programmes. Generation gaps close quickly and genuine friendships are made in the classrooms or the playcentre when older volunteers sit reading an afternoon story or helping out with a craft project.

Research undertaken by RSVP and carried out by older volunteers shows that most people are keen to take part and get involved in their community; they just need to be asked. Over 80% of older people who volunteer feel that they are making a real contribution to their communities. Over half have fun in the process.

Increasingly, CSV proves how its policy of community involvement can be applied across the spectrum of social care. Through CSV Education's partnership with over 3000 schools CSV encourages young people in full-time education to become active citizens and serve their community as part of their studies.

The nationwide programme of student tutoring, CSV Learning Together brings the enthusiasm and experience of undergraduates into the classrooms. The idea is a simple one. Students from over 80 universities volunteer to work alongside teachers for an afternoon a week, helping pupils with their studies, raising their aspirations and encouraging them to on to higher education.

Across the airwaves, CSV has pioneered social action broadcasting since the mid-seventies, forging innovative and adventurous working partnerships with over 40 BBC and independent radio and television stations across the country and in Europe. CSV Media informs millions of people every year and energises them to take action in their communities.

T R A V E L   A D V I C E

Some volunteer-sending agencies will organise all the travel arrangements for their volunteers, but if you are travelling independently there is one travel agency which complements the theme of this book, as its profits contribute to the funds of charities working in the developing world. North-South Travel Ltd are based at Moulsham Mill Parkway, Chelmsford, Essex CM2 7PX ✆ Chelmsford (0245) 492882, and they arrange competitively priced, reliably planned flights to most parts of the world.

Other agencies which specialise in cheap student/youth airfares include Campus Travel, 52 Grosvenor Gardens, London SW1W 0AG ✆ 071-730 8111 and STA Travel, 74 Old Brompton Road, London SW7 3LQ ✆ 071-937 9962. Both these agencies have branches throughout the UK, often on student campuses. Campus Travel's partner company in Ireland is USIT, whose head office is at O'Connell Bridge, 19-21 Aston Quay, Dublin 2 ✆ Dublin (01) 778117.

Trailfinders also operate low-cost flights between London and destinations worldwide, and will offer plenty of helpful advice to travellers in planning their trip. Their travel centre in London, based at 42-50 Earls Court Road, London W8 6EJ ✆ 071-938 3366 also has a travellers' library and information centre, an immunisation centre for overseas travel vaccinations, a travel goods shop and a map/bookshop.

If you are really shopping around for a cheap flight it pays to do careful research, checking with travel agencies such as those listed above and also with major airlines to find out what sort of deals they have available, before booking at a bucket shop. Don't part with any money before ensuring that the agency is a member of the Association of British Travel Agencies (ABTA) or the International Association of Travel Agents (IATA) and holds an Air Travel Organisers' Licence (ATOL).

Always double-check your travel details such as flight number, time of departure, check-in time and any Customs regulations that apply. It is very easy to forget small but important things: for example you may have to pay airport or departure taxes, so find out whether these are included in the ticket price, and if not, in which currency they are payable. If you've booked a flight some time in advance, don't forget to confirm the booking a day or two before departure.

Visas For entry to some countries a visa or visitor's pass is required. The recruiting agency should inform you about entry and exit visa procedures, but it is always wise to check for yourself whether a visa is required and that you obtain one that is valid for the length of time you expect to be in the country. If you plan to do any extensive travelling, investigate the possibility of getting a multiple entry visa. You can get information on visas from the consular section of the relevant embassy, but make sure you allow yourself plenty of time, as the visa application process can be a lengthy one.

Passports It is essential to check that your passport is valid at least for the time you intend to stay overseas and, as your circumstances may change, it is wise to allow an extra six months. Immigration and other government officials usually turn to a new page when stamping passports, so check that there are enough clear pages for visas and stamps; the British Passport Office issues a 94-page passport which is useful for those doing a lot of travelling through several countries. Always apply at least three months in advance for a passport, especially in the holiday season; a standard UK passport costs £15 (£22.50 if particulars of family are included), the larger size costs £30. Both are valid for 10 years and are obtainable from the following regional offices:

Passport Office, Clive House, 70-78 Petty France, London SW1H 9HD ✆ 071-279 3434 (personal callers only).

Passport Office, 5th Floor, India Buildings, Water Street, Liverpool L2 0QZ ✆ 051-237 3010

Passport Office, Olympia House, Upper Dock Street, Newport, Gwent NP9 1XA ✆ Newport (0633) 244500

Passport Office, Aragon Court, Northminster Road, Peterborough, Cambridgeshire PE1 1QG ✆ Peterborough (0733) 895555

Passport Office, 3 Northgate, 96 Milton Street, Cowcaddens, Glasgow G4 0BT ✆ 041-332 0271

Passport Office, Hampton House, 47-53 High Street, Belfast BT1 2QS ✆ Belfast (0232) 232371

Nationals of other countries will need to consult their own passport-issuing authorities as to the issuing and validity of passports. If a passport is lost or stolen while abroad the local police should be notified immediately; if necessary your nearest embassy or consulate will issue a substitute. It is therefore wise to keep a separate note of your passport number.

The *Essential Information* booklet contains notes on illness or injury while abroad, insurance, vaccinations, NHS medical cards, consular assistance overseas, British Customs and other useful advice, and is available from all passport offices.

Health Some volunteer-sending agencies will provide in-country medical treatment, but it is still a sensible precaution to have thorough medical and dental check-ups well before you leave. If you need to take prescribed drugs then you must find out beforehand whether these are subject to any regulations in the country or countries to which you will be travelling - some medicines freely available in Britain may be strictly controlled in other countries. A letter from your doctor giving details of any prescribed drugs can help in preventing any misunderstandings. Brand names for drugs vary from country to country, so find out the generic name for any prescribed drugs in case you need to get more whilst overseas. If you wear spectacles take a spare pair and make a note of the prescription in case you lose them. Contact lenses can prove to be painful and hard to keep clean in dusty regions, in which case you may wish to consider changing to spectacles.

Changes in food and climate may cause minor illnesses and, especially when visiting the hotter countries of southern Europe, North Africa, Latin America and the Far East, it is wise to take extra care in your hygiene, eating and drinking habits. Native bacteria, to which local inhabitants are immune, may cause the visitor stomach upsets, so it is worth avoiding tap water and doing without ice in your drinks.

In a hot climate never underestimate the strength of the sun, nor overestimate your own strength. Drink plenty of fluid, make sure there is enough salt in your diet, wear loose-fitting cotton clothes, even a hat, and guard against heat exhaustion, heat stroke and sunburn, especially if you are working outdoors.

Whilst abroad it is unwise to have your skin pierced by acupuncture, tattooing or ear piercing, for example, unless you can be sure that the equipment is sterile. A major cause of the spread of viruses, including AIDS, is the use of infected needles and equipment. In some countries blood for transfusions is not screened for the presence of the AIDS virus, but there may be arrangements for obtaining screened blood. The doctor treating you, or the nearest consulate or embassy may be able to offer advice.

If you are concerned about the availability of sterile equipment whilst abroad, emergency medical travel kits are available through MASTA (see the *Immunisations* section below) and other suppliers, and can be ordered through retail pharmacists. They contain a variety of sterilised and sealed items such as syringes and needles for use in emergencies. MASTA also has a range of health care items such as mosquito nets and water purifiers.

In the UK the Department of Health issues leaflet T4 *Health Advice for Travellers*, available from post offices, travel agents, libraries and doctors' surgeries, or by phoning 0800 555777. This includes details of compulsory and recommended vaccinations, other measures that can be taken to protect one's health, information on rabies, AIDS, malaria and other diseases. There is also advice on types of food and on water supplies which may be a source of infection.

A person is only covered by the NHS while in the UK, and will usually have to pay the full costs of any treatment abroad. However, there are health care arrangements between all EC countries (Belgium, Britain, Denmark, France, Germany, Greece, Ireland, Italy, Luxembourg, the Netherlands, Portugal and Spain). British citizens resident in the UK will receive free or reduced cost emergency treatment in other EC countries on production of form E111 which is included inside leaflet T4, see above.

Leaflet T4 also explains who is covered by the arrangements, what treatment is free or at reduced cost, and gives the procedures which must be followed to get treatment in countries where form E111 is not needed (usually Denmark, Ireland and Portugal). Form E111 must be taken abroad and, if emergency treatment is needed, the correct procedures must be followed.

There are also reciprocal health care arrangements between Britain and Australia, Austria, Barbados, Bulgaria, Channel Islands, Czechoslovakia, Finland, Gibraltar, Hong Kong, Hungary, Iceland, Isle of Man, Malta, New Zealand, Norway, Poland, Romania, Sweden, former republics of the USSR, Yugoslavia and the British Dependent Territories of Anguilla, British Virgin Islands, Falkland Islands, Montserrat, St Helena, and Turks and Caicos Islands. However, private health insurance may still be needed in these countries; leaflet T4 gives full details.

Despite reciprocal health arrangements it is still *essential* to ensure you have full medical insurance cover whenever travelling overseas. The health treatment available in other countries may not be as comprehensive as in the UK, and *none* of the arrangements listed above cover the cost of repatriation in the event of illness.

Immunisation Immunisation should be started well in advance, as some courses necessitate an interval between the first and second inoculation, or between one immunisation and another. With vaccination against yellow fever, for example, there must be an interval of at least 21 days before any other vaccination with a live virus, such as polio. Also, as immunity may take several days to develop, validity may not be immediate - immigration officials will not accept a yellow fever immunisation certificate until 10 days after the vaccination. And, as you may suffer after-effects from a vaccination it is sensible to allow yourself time to recover before you leave, rather than suffering during the journey and the first few days abroad.

A certificate of vaccination against certain diseases (usually cholera and yellow fever) is an entry requirement for some countries, and it is best to consult embassies on this point, since requirements are continually subject to review. Other immunisations are merely recommended, but may well be even more vital to your health. These include tetanus - especially if you will be doing manual work outdoors; typhoid - particularly important in the tropics; polio - have a booster if it's 10 years since you were last vaccinated; hepatitis - many volunteer agencies will insist on your being immunised; rabies - for those at special risk such as vets and zoologists; and malaria - currently one of the worst health hazards for British travellers to Africa, Asia and Latin America.

The volunteer-sending agency may be able to advise you on appropriate vaccinations. Up-to-date printouts indicating the immunisations and malaria tablets appropriate for any specific journey are also available at a cost of £5 payable by credit card from the Medical Advisory Service to Travellers Abroad (MASTA) ② 071-631 4408 or 0705 511420. Be prepared to give the countries to be visited in a journey (up to 6) in sequence, the month of arrival in each and the living conditions (rural, towns, cities, business, tourist), and the required information will be sent by return. MASTA printouts are also available without charge for those attending British Airways Travel Clinics for their immunisations; for details of the clinic nearest to you ② 071-831 5333.

Insurance It is in your own interests to have adequate insurance, not only for medical treatment, but also life and personal accident cover and to cover cash and possessions. Many volunteer-sending agencies do provide insurance, but this may only be against third party risks and accidents, in which case you will need to supplement the provision. You may already have an insurance policy covering you both at home and overseas, but this may need extending to cover the nature of the situation in which you will find yourself as a volunteer. It is common to include cover in the policy for ambulance transport and in certain circumstances repatriation, including medical attention on the journey and the conveyance of a relative or friend. Cover for personal effects should include baggage in transit and at destination, and expensive individual items such as photographic equipment. Check carefully the limit for the total package as well as for each claim, make sure that the policy does cover you for the type work that you will be doing, and find out whether there is a representative of the insurance company in the destination country to whom claims can be made.

Whatever insurance cover you take out, do make sure that you read the small print very thoroughly before you travel, and take a copy of the policy with you, keeping a separate note of the policy number. If a claim needs to be made then the insurance company should be informed of all the details without delay, and where a crime is involved the local police must also be notified.

National Insurance The regulations covering National Insurance contributions and social security are complex and become more complicated for those paying contributions while overseas. Your entitlement to sickness, invalidity and unemployment benefit, maternity allowance, and state pension is governed by your National Insurance record, but this does not affect entitlement to other social security benefits such as income support. Some agencies, including those funded by the British Government, will automatically pay National Insurance contributions for their volunteers (see information below about VDW contributions), but whichever organisation you are working with it is essential to clarify the position regarding National Insurance contributions well in advance of taking up a post; neglecting to make proper arrangements may well prejudice any future claims for benefits.

If you are going to one of the EC countries, leaflet SA29, *Your social security, health care and pension rights in the European Community*, available from the Department of Social Security, Overseas Contributions Agency, see below, gives details of National Insurance contributions, plus the social security rights available to UK nationals and how and where to claim them.

If you are going outside the EC, there are separate leaflets detailing social security procedures in countries with which the UK has a reciprocal arrangement: Australia, Austria, Barbados, Bermuda, Canada, Croatia, Cyprus, Finland, Iceland, Israel, Jamaica, Jersey and Guernsey, Malta, Mauritius, New Zealand, Norway, Philippines, Slovenia, Sweden, Switzerland, Turkey, United States and the Federal Republic of Yugoslavia. For other countries, leaflet NI38, *Social Security abroad* applies.

From 6 April 1986 a special Volunteer Development Worker (VDW) contribution was introduced, and can be paid by volunteers going abroad where the following conditions apply: the volunteer normally lives in the United Kingdom, is recruited by an approved organisation, and has gone overseas to work in a recognised developing country. The VDW contribution in most cases is paid direct to the Overseas Contributions Agency by the recruiting organisation; however it is possible in some cases for volunteers to make their own payment arrangements. The payment of VDW contributions will normally provide cover for sickness and unemployment benefit following a person's return to the UK provided the contribution years on which the claim is assessed are covered by the absence abroad.

For copies of leaflets mentioned above and any further information, contact the Contributions Agency, Overseas Contributions, Department of Social Security, Newcastle upon Tyne NE98 1YX.

Emergencies Find out before you leave what support the volunteer-sending agency can give you in times of emergency or trouble. Many organisations have country representatives or field officers who will at least act as a point of contact between volunteers and the sending agency.

The British Consulate or the Consular Section of British Embassies or High Commissions

will be able to offer advice and help,
especially if there is no-one else to turn to, but
do consider other options such as the local
police or a local representative of your bank
or insurance company. If you do need help
from the Consulate, try to phone or telegraph
in advance; the telegraphic address of all
British Embassies is *Prodrome* and of all
British Consulates *Britain*, followed in each
case by the name of the town. Consuls will
advise or help in cases of serious difficulty or
distress; they cannot give advice on, or pay
for, legal proceedings, but will do what they
can to help in such cases. As a last resort, and
in exceptional circumstances, they can,
providing strict conditions are met, make a
repayable loan for repatriation to the UK.

Before you go overseas, make sure that you
have the following information, kept separate
from your other belongings: passport number,
date and place of issue; travel ticket numbers,
dates and places of issue; insurance details
and 24-hour emergency number; local agency
or representative details; Embassy or
Consulate contact address and phone number;
serial numbers of travellers' cheques; any
medical prescriptions or doctor's instructions.

RETURNING   HOME

Some six months before the end of the assignment you should begin to prepare yourself for the return home. The sending agency should be ready to help and advise on resettlement, and you should request information about job openings and other practical matters whilst still overseas. Many volunteers find the culture shock of returning home equal to that of going; those who come back not expecting to meet practical problems concerning health, housing, employment and state benefits can find themselves under considerable stress.

As indicated in the entries throughout *Volunteer Work*, many agencies arrange debriefings. In some cases these can be fairly perfunctory, but those agencies who are genuinely concerned for the welfare of their development workers will give you the opportunity to report back and evaluate the project in which you have taken part. In this way you can begin to effectively utilise the experience gained overseas: by pointing out successful methods, drawing attention to failures and describing the working conditions your reports and comments will be able to aid the agency in its work in the future. Another way in which you can apply what you have learnt abroad is to take part in briefing courses for prospective volunteers, speaking to trainees about your experience, offering advice and practical information.

Two years or so of working overseas, especially as a development worker in the Third World, is bound to change you in many ways. You will have seen things from a different perspective and your views on development and underdevelopment, and the role played by industrialised countries may have sharpened somewhat, to say nothing of the fresh eye with which you will view your home surroundings. If your experience urges you to carry on working for development from home, then check the *Understanding Development* section for organisations who would appreciate your help in their work towards raising people's awareness about development issues. The agency that send you abroad in the first place may also put you in touch with development organisations, or they may even help you set up a development education project.

Learning to learn from the South is the theme of the Manchester-based project where Celia Marshall works:

You'll often hear returned volunteers saying that they gained more than they gave when they went overseas. After three years as a volunteer in Ghana, I definitely fall into that category. I went to share my skills, as the VSO motto says, but I returned to Britain a good deal wiser about the meaning of sharing.

When I came home I felt very strongly about the need for development education, but not so much on a political level - looking at why famine occurs and how much money the South 'owes' Northern banks - as on a personal level. I felt it should be about people in the UK learning from people from the South; and people from the South living in Britain being valued for the contribution they can make here, and welcomed as brothers and sisters, as I was when I lived in Ghana.

The Southern Voices Project, where I now work full-time, is a start. Set up in 1990 through a VSO Development Education Award, it seeks to involve people from the South who are living and studying in the Manchester area with schools, community groups, workshops and conferences, and to create opportunities where people can learn from each other. I work as part of a team of overseas students and community workers, talking to people, making links and offering support.

In all the contact we arrange, the emphasis is on the human dimension. For example, Kwame, a Ghanaian student in Manchester, has spoken to a group of students on how the debt crisis is affecting ordinary people in Ghana. Martha, from Ecuador, has made several visits to a primary school to talk to children about her country and culture - they learned games, listened to stories and cooked an Ecuadorian meal together.

I hope that the Southern Voices Project will continue to make a contribution - even if only a small one - to helping people here in the North learn how to receive from the South with an eagerness equal to their desire to give. Until we are open to receiving, we will be unable to share.

Further help on advice, resettlement, reorientation and continuing commitment can be obtained from the following organisations:

AVEC 155a Kings Road, Chelsea, London SW3 5TX ✆ 071-352 2033
A service agency for church and community development which organises residential courses, sponsored partly by the Methodist and Roman Catholic Churches, for missionaries returning to work in the UK and Ireland. Open to ordained and lay people of all denominations, the courses provide opportunities to reflect on what has been learnt from missionary experience and to draw out the practical and theological implications for the work to be taken up in the UK and for the sponsoring missionary organisation.

CHRISTIANS ABROAD 1 Stockwell Green, London SW9 9HP ✆ 071-737 7811
An ecumenical body, founded in 1972 and supported by aid and mission agencies. Organises one-day *Back to Britain* workshops for groups of people who have recently returned from working overseas. Sessions include pictures of an experience; the coming back occasion; and the next step. Staff work

with groups of 4-10 people to acknowledge the joys, frustrations, hopes and fears that were part of the overseas experience; affirm what has been learned from that experience; consider the process of returning to Britain; affirm experience as a resource for paid and unpaid work in Britain; and consider the stumbling blocks and supports for sharing what has been learned overseas with others in Britain.

COMHLAMH 61 Lower Camden Street, Dublin 2, Ireland ☎ Dublin (01) 783490 Fax (01) 783738
The Returned Development Workers' Association of Ireland aims to maintain friendship and partnership with the peoples of the developing countries; to contribute to a greater awareness on the part of the Irish people of the problems of developing countries and of solutions required; to assist returning development workers with their readjustment to life in Ireland and in obtaining employment; and to assist them to contribute effectively from their experience in social and community development in Ireland. Its activities are carried out through local branches and groups that focus on distinct development issues. The Services' Group in particular helps workers by providing them with reorientation weekends, communications skills courses, practical guidance concerning jobs, retraining and social welfare benefits and information about possibilities for development work in Ireland. Publishes *Focus, Ireland and the Wider World* quarterly magazine, and a development education newsletter, *Node News*.

RETURNED VOLUNTEER ACTION 1 Amwell Street, London EC1R 1UL ☎ 071-278 0804
An organisation of, and for, serving and returned volunteers, those interested or active in development work, and others who have worked overseas. It believes that a period of voluntary service overseas fails to achieve its full value unless it becomes part of an educative process for the volunteer, and much of its work involves face-to-face contact between more recently returned volunteers and those who have been back for up to two years. Its main aims are to press for improvements in the volunteer programme and help returned volunteers evaluate their overseas experience, using the understanding which that experience has given them in development education, community action and other fields in the UK.

Practical advice and support is provided in reorientation days; other conferences on development education themes are held from time to time, and returned volunteers are helped in their search for work in the UK with a Jobsheet in the members' quarterly magazine *Comeback*. Members participate in local activities wherever they can and in many areas have themselves taken initiatives in starting development orientated activities. In addition to its Volunteer Policy, Development Education, Publications and other Groups, RVA actively supports small development projects overseas through a Development Fund.

RVA publishes a range of titles including a *Working Overseas* advisory pack containing information on the sending agencies and general information for the prospective overseas worker/volunteer; *Working For Development in London; Questioning Development; Handbook for Development Workers Overseas; Thinking About Volunteering; EVI Charter;* and *For Whose Benefit?*

B R I N G I N G   I T   A L L   B A C K   H O M E

Many volunteers find the culture shock of returning home equal to that of going, and without the right preparation may find themselves under great stress. The first part of effectively utilising the experiences gained overseas is to engage in construction evaluation of the project. Returned volunteers should also take up any opportunity to participate in briefing courses for prospective volunteers, being able to provide a range of alternative reference points. All too often returned volunteers find that the opportunities to apply what has been learnt abroad to life and work in the home country are limited. Alex Lipinski of Returned Volunteer Action, an organisation of, and for, returned volunteers, here outlines some of the problems to be faced by the returning volunteer.

Coming back home after two years abroad can be as much a jolt to the system as going out in the first place, and can cause as many problems for the unprepared. The experience of living in a totally different country and culture often changes the way returnees view their own country, and the issue of fitting in again is a concern common to returned volunteers. Sometimes there is the problem of a lack of money, or having to look for work or somewhere to live again. Or the problem may be a difficulty in adjusting to the pace of life again, perhaps even trying to avoid becoming a volunteer bore to friends.

Eleanor Kercher spent two years teaching in Africa before arriving back in 1990:

People expect you to fit straight back in. They ask you how was Africa and expect a two minute answer. After that they aren't interested. Also the culture shock - things like going into a fully stocked supermarket and seeing the waste. Those kinds of things are important as they build up quickly when you return. It made me feel alienated. I wasn't interested in what people had to say about their houses, because I wanted to talk about the amazing experience I had. Basically for most people it is so out of their way that they don't know how to react to it.

Although volunteers are given extensive training before they leave home, Eleanor wishes her sending agency had been more supportive on her return:

It's a very solitary thing coming back. You've been through this massive experience, then you come home and have to pick up the pieces again. It's different to when you go out, lots of orientation programmes and training, but coming back you get off the plane and - nothing.

Aled Williams was more fortunate:

My social network was quite strong when I returned and I got the support I wanted. Maybe I would have felt different if I was single with no close family.

He also feels the time spent abroad is itself a preparation for coping with resettlement:

People who go out to a developing country are resourceful and self-reliant; they develop these abilities out there so when they came back they should adopt a similar kind of approach to problems.

These days the support services available to returnees are much better. VSO for instance has a returned volunteer office which provides information and advice for its returning volunteers, who may be considering a career change or wish to become more involved in development work. Returned Volunteer Action, too, gives advice to returned development workers from any sending agency in the UK and can put them in touch with local support groups. Despite problems, Eleanor is enthusiastic about the benefits of volunteering:

The most useful thing about it is the experience that you bring back. The effect of your two years work abroad is tiny compared to the effect it has on you. Just living in a totally different culture makes you able to look at your own culture and question its values. I feel that I can now be more effective in working for development in this country.

Aled also sees positive benefits:

The experience has given me the confidence to work anywhere abroad, even under my own steam, without the support of an organisation.

It can take some time, up to a year even, before returnees start to settle down and consider their future. Says Eleanor:

A lot of people wish to do something completely different when they come back. Particularly in the present economic climate that's often very difficult. It's also difficult to get back into your own professional field because things have moved on. Often employers think you've taken a two year holiday and your experience isn't relevant.

Rather than changing her career, Eleanor worked her experience into her teaching:

My first idea was to go back abroad immediately but then I realised it would jeopardise any education work I wanted to do. I also wanted to get into development work, but it's a very small field with many people wanting to do it, so I went back to teaching. But things have changed in that I do a lot of development education in school, and because I trained teachers abroad I now run more training courses than I would otherwise.

Aled incorporated his volunteering experience into his career plans. He saw it as an essential part of his professional development:

It's important that the post you go out to contributes to your professional development, otherwise you gain only the social development skills which though necessary, employers don't always value.

SECTION V

VOLUNTARY SERVICE:

RECRUITING

AGENCIES

A C T I O N   H E A L T H   2 0 0 0

Information Officer, Action Health 2000, 25 Gwydir Street, Cambridge CB1 2LG

Cambridge (0223) 460853

India, Tanzania, Zambia, Zimbabwe

Founded in 1984, Action Health 2000 is an international voluntary health association with no political or religious affiliations, working for better health care in Asia and Africa by creating greater awareness of the issues involved and giving practical support to appropriate health programmes. Its general purpose is to work towards the World Health Organisation's target of making basic health care accessible to the world's poorest peoples. In addition, Action Health 2000 provides and encourages links between health professionals worldwide, and is concerned with health care research and education.

International Study & Training Programme allows doctors, nurses, midwives, health visitors, physio and speech therapists and other health personnel to work as volunteers in rural, semi-rural or deprived urban areas. Recruits 20 health professionals annually.

Ages 21+. Appropriate professional health qualifications necessary. No experience necessary on application, though selected individuals may be asked to acquire specific experience before being sent overseas. Applicants should be resourceful, resilient, sensitive to local cultures and difficulties, compassionate and understanding, and have non-verbal communication skills. A multi-disciplinary approach and the ability to work as part of a team required. Volunteers only accepted after satisfactory medical report. All nationalities considered. PH

6 months-2 years

Simple housing, adequate local food, insurance, travel costs and £30-£60 pocket money per month provided. Participants contribute approx £750 of total costs, but this and pocket money vary depending on project/length of service. Advice given on sponsorship.

Shortlisted applicants can meet former volunteers at selection weekends. Compulsory, comprehensive 3 day orientation course arranged. Language training is given. Returned volunteers are debriefed and provided with help and advice on resettlement and finding a job, and are encouraged to participate in the society's UK activities.

Recruitment all year; usually a 6-12 month gap between application and departure

Newsletter; project reports; information leaflets

AFRICA   INLAND   MISSION

Assistant Personnel Secretary, Africa Inland Mission, 2 Vorley Road, Archway, London N19 5HE

071-281 1184

Africa: mainly Kenya, but other countries as needs arise

AIM is a Protestant missionary society whose aims are evangelism and church planting

There are opportunities for teaching in rural schools and working with young people. Some 30 volunteers are recruited each year.

Ages 18-70. Applicants must have A levels or a degree for teaching. Knowledge of French helpful for some countries. All applicants must be committed Christians with a desire to serve God in Africa.

One year, departing end of August

Housing is provided but volunteers are required to raise all their travel expenses, insurance, living allowances and administration costs through their churches and Christian friends. Advice is given on obtaining sponsorship.

Compulsory orientation course provided. One-day debriefing seminar on return.

Apply September-May

AIM *International* quarterly magazine

AGENCY FOR PERSONAL SERVICE OVERSEAS

Overseas Register, Agency for Personal Service Overseas, 30 Fitzwilliam Square, Dublin 2, Ireland

Dublin (01) 614411   Fax (01) 614202

Over 40 developing countries, mainly, but not exclusively, in Africa

A state-sponsored body established in 1974 to promote and sponsor temporary personal service in the developing countries of the world for their economic and social development, in the interests of justice and peace among nations. It co-funds volunteers with other sending agencies, recruits on behalf of governments and non-governmental agencies in developing countries, and seeks to protect the interest of development workers on their return.

Volunteers are needed in the areas of education, medicine, engineering/construction, agriculture, administration and social sciences. There are vacancies for doctors, nurses, pharmacists, physiotherapists, nutritionists and medical laboratory technicians; teachers of English, science, maths, primary education, home economics, secretarial/commercial skills and technical subjects; university lecturers; mechanical, civil and electrical engineers; carpenters and mechanics; horticulturalists and agriculturalists; administrators and project managers; social workers and community development specialists. Recruits and funds approx 400 volunteers annually.

Ages 21+. Applicants must be Irish nationals. Basic skills or qualifications required. Experience preferred but not essential. Applicants must have a genuine interest in helping a developing country. B D PH W subject to placement opportunities.

Normally 2 years

Return airfares, insurance, accommodation and living allowance provided

Orientation, professional skills training and language courses provided. Re-orientation days organised by Comhlámh, who maintain a job register for returning development workers.

Recruitment all year

Annual Report, training brochure, newsletter

A S S O C I A T E   M I S S I O N A R I E S   O F T H E   A S S U M P T I O N

The Director, Assumption Convent, 227 N Bowman Avenue, Merion, Pennsylvania 19066, United States

(215) 664 1284

West and East Africa, Japan, Argentina, United States and Europe: France, Spain, Germany, Italy and the UK

Founded in 1960, provides lay men and women with the opportunity to share their skills with others in teaching, medical work or towards the development of peoples in another country

Volunteers are needed to teach at elementary and secondary level; or to live and work in communities for people with mental handicaps, retirement homes or nursing centres.

Ages 22-45. College graduates or equivalent preferred. Previous volunteer experience essential. Applicants should have a deep faith, generosity, forgetfulness of self, the ability to adapt to new cultures and the willingness to tackle any job they are given. Knowledge of relevant languages helpful.

One year minimum

Board and lodging provided, plus health insurance and stipend of approx $100 per month. One-way fare provided for a one year commitment, return fare for a two year commitment.

Compulsory orientation course arranged prior to departure; plus re-entry weekend on return

Apply by 15 March

ASSOCIATES OF MILL HILL MISSIONARIES

Associate Secretary, Associates of Mill Hill Missionaries, St Joseph's Missionary Society, St Joseph's College, Lawrence Street, Mill Hill, London NW7 4JX

081-959 8254

Africa: Cameroon, Kenya, Sudan, Uganda, Zaire; Asia: Pakistan; Latin America: Chile, Falkland Islands

The work of the Mill Hill Missionaries goes back to the late 19th century and since 1970 associate lay members have joined the service to work with the priests and brothers. The organisation enables lay missionaries to use their talents and skills to build up God's people in mission lands, and to channel and employ the gifts of many for the service of the missionary ideal.

Vacancies exist in the areas of teaching, nursing, social and pastoral work, catechetics, engineering and building work in a missionary context

Ages 21+. Applicants must have Christian and missionary motivation, relevant professional or technical qualifications and skills, and at least 2 years' work experience. Some form of experience doing voluntary or parish work is recommended. The ability to work as part of an international team and the maturity to adapt oneself to different cultures and work in isolated conditions are also important. All nationalities considered; working knowledge of English essential.

Three years

Board and lodging, insurance, travel costs and local missionary allowance provided

Introductory weekends held regularly for those interested in applying. Compulsory three month preparatory course organised in England and the Netherlands before Associates take up their placements. Oral debriefing arranged on return, plus financial assistance until a job has been found.

Recruitment all year

Two booklets: *A Century of Charity - The Story of the Mill Hill Missionaries*; *The Changing Face of Mission*

ATD FOURTH WORLD

The General Secretary, ATD Fourth World, 48 Addington Square, London SE5 7LB

Africa: Burkina Faso, Central African Republic, Ivory Coast, Madagascar, Mauritius, Reunion, Senegal
Asia: Philippines, Thailand, Sri Lanka
Europe: Belgium, Britain, France, Germany, Luxembourg, Netherlands, Spain, Switzerland
Latin America: Guatemala, Haiti, Honduras
North America: Canada, United States

An international human rights organisation founded in 1957 in France. Aims to explore all possibilities of partnership with the most disadvantaged families who constitute the Fourth World and to encourage private citizens and public officials to join this effort.

Volunteers spend time at ATD's international centre in France before becoming part of a team. Volunteers run programmes in the heart of very poor communities, building on the strengths and hopes of these families. They provide a forum for the disadvantaged and ensure that the voice of the Fourth World is heard at local, national and international levels.

Ages 18+. There are no professional or academic requirements; everyone is welcome. Applicants should have a genuine interest in learning from the experiences and hopes of very disadvantaged communities as a vital first step to building a future with them, and a willingness to work hard with others in a team. Those interested in becoming long-term volunteers can find out more about the organisation through working weekends, international workcamps or summer street-library programmes. Further details about these opportunities are given in *Working Holidays*.

After a 3 month placement volunteers who want to stay on are expected to make a 1 or 2 year commitment

Volunteers are required to pay their food expenses for the first month; for the following 2 months food and accommodation is provided. People who stay on are paid in increments up to the minimum salary which all permanent volunteers receive after 1 year. Accident insurance provided.

Volunteers receive a full introduction into the work of ATD Fourth World

Recruitment all year

BAPTIST MISSIONARY SOCIETY

The Candidate Secretary, Baptist Missionary Society, PO Box 49, Baptist House, Didcot, Oxon OX11 8XA

Didcot (0235) 512077

Africa: Angola, Zaire; Asia: Bangladesh, India, Nepal, Sri Lanka, Thailand
Caribbean: Jamaica, Trinidad
Europe: Belgium, France, Italy
Latin America: Brazil, El Salvador, Nicaragua

An organisation of Baptist churches in the UK, aiming for the diffusion of the religion of Jesus Christ throughout the world. Works in partnership with churches overseas.

BMS gets involved in the evangelistic work of the local church. Projects may include church-planting; social projects such as running a day-care nursery for young children; agricultural and development schemes; education and vocational teaching; medical assistance; training and pastoral work; and supporting national Christians in their work and ministry. There are two types of placement: long-term for students furthering their studies, for example in medical work, engineering or teaching; also BMS Action Teams involving young people in short-term missionary work.

Ages 18-30 for Action Teams, 18+ for volunteers. No experience or qualifications necessary for Action Teams. Long-term volunteers must have qualifications relevant to the task they wish to undertake. All applicants must have a clear call from God, be involved in their local Baptist church and committed to the expansion of God's kingdom on earth.

Action Teams: 1-3 month summer programme or 9 month placement departing October, which includes training, 6 months abroad and 3 months touring Baptist churches in Britain presenting what was done overseas. Volunteers: typically 6-12 months.

Board and lodging provided. Small amount of pocket money for Action Teams. All participants are encouraged to pay as much as possible towards travel expenses.

Training and debriefing provided

Apply well in advance for Action Teams. Volunteers: recruitment all year.

Missionary Herald monthly; *Look!* monthly (for children); information leaflets

BCMS CROSSLINKS

The International Secretary, BCMS Crosslinks, 251 Lewisham Way, London SE4 1XF

081-691 6111

Africa: Kenya, Tanzania, Uganda, Zimbabwe
Europe: France, Portugal, Russia, Spain
Latin America: Bolivia, Peru

Founded in 1922 as the Bible Churchmen's Missionary Society, BCMS Crosslinks is an evangelical missionary society of the Church of England, working in partnership with all branches of the Anglican Communion overseas. Their motto is *God's Word to God's World*, reflecting their commitment to the Bible and to the international nature of mission. There is an increasing awareness of mission being a crosslinking of men and women, old and young, rich and poor in every continent.

Requests from overseas churches are for accountants, administrators, agriculturists, Bible teachers, evangelists, primary and secondary teachers, doctors, student workers, and people skilled in broadcasting, bookselling and literature production.

Ages 21+; most volunteers are in their late 20s. Volunteers should have a commitment to Jesus Christ as Saviour and Lord, a sense of God's call and a willingness to work in partnership with the overseas church as a dedicated servant of God. Qualifications and experience in an appropriate field required. Professional, and often postgraduate qualifications needed for medical and teaching personnel. Knowledge/study of languages required as appropriate. All nationalities considered.

Two years minimum

Most overseas institutions and dioceses provide basic accommodation but not food. Monthly allowance is designed to provide a reasonable standard of living. National Insurance contributions and travel provided.

Training at All Nations Christian College or a similar institution desirable but not essential. Consultation with one of the Regional Coordinators provided as debriefing.

Recruitment all year

Mission quarterly magazine; *Crosslinks* newsletter

BEANNACHAR LTD

Elisabeth Phethean, Housemother, Beannachar, Banchory-Devenick, Aberdeen AB1 5YL

Aberdeen (0224) 861825/868605

Outskirts of Aberdeen

Camphill community for further education and training, with the aims of providing meaningful work and a home for young adults with varying degrees of handicap or disturbance

Volunteers are required to help care for students and work with them on a communal basis. Work involves gardening, cooking, building, cleaning, looking after animals, laundry, weaving and woodwork. Volunteers are also expected to participate in other community activities such as folk dancing, drama, festivals, walking, swimming, games and outings.

Ages 19+. Volunteers should be enthusiastic, caring and willing to learn, with a sense of responsibility and initiative. No previous experience or qualifications necessary.

6-12+ months; some short-term summer placements available

Volunteers work a 6 day week and receive £18 per week pocket money, plus full board and lodging in the community. Hours are approx 0630-2130. Students and staff live together in 2 large family units. Volunteers staying longer than 12 months have return journey home paid.

Recruitment all year

BRETHREN VOLUNTEER SERVICE

The Recruitment Officer, Brethren Volunteer Service, 1451 Dundee Avenue, Elgin, Illinois 60120, United States

(708) 742 5100

United States and limited opportunities in the Caribbean: Haiti, Puerto Rico, Virgin Islands;   Europe: France, Germany, Ireland, Netherlands, Northern Ireland, Poland, Switzerland;   Latin America: Bolivia, Chile, Ecuador, El Salvador, Honduras, Mexico, Nicaragua, Uruguay;   China, Egypt and Israel.

A Christian service programme founded in 1948, dedicated to advocating justice, peacemaking and serving basic human needs. BVS is characterised by the spirit of sharing God's love through acts of service and reflects the heritage of reconciliation and service of the Church of the Brethren, its sponsoring denomination.

There are over 200 projects, some dealing with immediate needs, others working towards changing unjust systems; the range of personnel is wide and constantly updated. Recent projects have needed agricultural workers, environmentalists, maintenance experts, construction supervisors, writers, drivers, cooks, craft workers, medical personnel, child care aides, social/youth workers, community organisers, instructors to the disabled, aides to the aged, peace/prison reform organisers, refugee resettlement coordinators, teachers and administrators.

Ages 18+. Applicants should be willing to act on their commitments and values; they will be challenged to offer themselves, their time and talents, to work that is both difficult and demanding. They are expected to study and examine the Christian faith, to be open to personal growth and willing to share in the lives of others. High school education or equivalent required. The programme especially needs those with relevant skills and experience, but also the less experienced if they bring a willingness to grow and a desire to learn. All nationalities considered. B D PH

1 year minimum for US; 2 years service elsewhere

Participants meet their own costs to orientation in the US; thereafter BVS provides travel, insurance and $45 per month allowance, which may be increased in the second year. Board and lodging provided in apartments/houses or occasionally with a family.

Compulsory 3 week orientation course when the project assignments are made with the input of BVS and the volunteer. There may be a waiting period between orientation and overseas assignment; interim assignments will be arranged. Debriefing provided during in-service retreat.

Apply at least 3 months in advance

BRITISH EXECUTIVE SERVICE OVERSEAS

Public Relations Manager, British Executive Service Overseas, 164 Vauxhall Bridge Road, London SW1V 2RB

071-630 0644

Fifty countries in the developing world, Eastern and Central Europe

An independent organisation, initiated by the Institute of Directors and established with the backing of the British Government and the Confederation of British Industry. The aims of the scheme are the advancement of industrial and commercial training and education in developing countries, Eastern and Central Europe; the improvement of managerial skills leading to greater efficiency in industry and commerce in these countries; the promotion of the science of supervisory management and organisation of systems and methods in the fields of industry, trade and commerce. BESO recruits executives by enlisting the help of employers, federations, professional institutes and trade associations, and maintains a register of executives.

Business people with industrial and commercial backgrounds are sent to advise small and medium-sized businesses on specific problems, sharing knowledge and expertise in a practical way with indigenous businesses and helping countries achieve economic independence, self-sustaining growth and a higher standard of living.

Volunteers should be retired business people or executives on secondment from their employers, with a successful record in the industrial or commercial fields. Applicants should have a commitment to passing on their skills; the level of expertise required depends on the individual assignment.

Average period 2-3 months; maximum usually 6 months

Travel, insurance and incidental expenses of the volunteer and spouse are met by BESO. Accommodation, subsistence and local transportation costs are borne by the requesting organisation.

Briefing provided on local conditions

Recruitment all year

Information leaflets; *BESO News* newsletter; *Annual Report*

CAMPHILL AM BODENSEE

Sekretariat, Camphill am Bodensee, Heimsonderschule Brachenreuthe, 7770 Überlingen-Bodensee, Germany

(07551) 80070

Near Überlingen, Germany

A residential school for mentally handicapped children, based near Lake Constance. The school cares for 90 children aged 4-17, and consists of 10 house communities, a therapy building, a community hall, a garden and a farm. Emphasis is placed on catering for the needs and problems of autistic children. The work is based on the teachings of Rudolf Steiner, and aims to help the children achieve individual independence within the Camphill Trust communities.

Volunteers are required to live and work with the children, helping out in classes and with bathing, dressing and other personal tasks. Volunteers are also encouraged to participate in the cultural, recreational and social aspects of community life.

Ages 19+. No previous experience or qualifications necessary. Volunteers should be caring, enthusiastic and willing to help wherever they are needed. A fairly good command of German is essential.

6-12+ months, usually starting mid August

Volunteers work a 6 day week, and have 5 weeks holiday in a year. Full board single/double room accommodation, insurance and DM350 per month pocket money provided. Volunteers pay their own travel expenses.

Those staying for a year have the opportunity to take part in a training course in curative education

Recruitment all year

Information leaflets

CAMPHILL RUDOLF STEINER SCHOOLS

Central Office, Camphill Rudolf Steiner Schools, Murtle Estate, Bieldside, Aberdeen AB1 9EP

Aberdeen (0224) 867935

Outside Aberdeen, Scotland

Founded in 1939 by the late Dr Karl König, the Camphill schools offer residential schooling and therapy, based on the teachings of Rudolf Steiner, for children and young adults in need of special care. Members of staff and their families live with the 155 pupils in 16 separate house communities on the three small estates that comprise the Schools' grounds.

Co-workers are required to live with children in family units, helping with the care of children and the running of the house and garden, and of the estate. Approx 80 volunteers are recruited each year.

Ages 20-40. No previous experience or qualifications required, but applicants should have an open mind and an interest in children, community life, curative education and anthroposophy.

Twelve months minimum, beginning August, late October, early January and late April

Co-workers receive board and lodging plus £20 per week pocket money. There is one day off each week, otherwise no separation between on and off duty. Return travel costs to home country (within Europe) provided after 1 year.

Orientation course provided

Recruitment all year; apply at least 6 months in advance

CAMPHILL SPECIAL SCHOOLS (BEAVER RUN)

Applications Group, Camphill Special Schools, RD1, Beaver Run, Glenmoore, Pennsylvania 19343, United States

Pennsylvania, United States

A children's village community of approx 150 people, of which nearly half are mentally handicapped children and adolescents

Volunteers are required to live and work in the community, caring for small groups of children in family homes and in the school, assisting in land work and craft activities such as weaving, woodwork and pottery

Ages 19-35. Some previous experience of work with children with or without mental handicaps is desirable. Volunteers should be enthusiastic and keen to learn.

One year placements from September-July preferred

Volunteers work approx 50 hours per week and are provided with board and lodging in a village home, plus approx $130 per month pocket money. Group medical and dental insurance provided. Student visa arranged but participants must pay their own travel costs.

Ongoing orientation for those new to the work

Apply 4-6 months in advance

CAMPHILL VILLAGE
KIMBERTON HILLS

The Admissions Group, Camphill Village Kimberton Hills, PO Box 155, Kimberton, Pennsylvania 19442, United States

(215) 935 0300

Pennsylvania, United States

An agricultural community based on a 430 acre estate in the rolling hills of southeast Pennsylvania. There is a total population of 130, including some 50 adults with mental handicaps. The community raises vegetables, grains, fruits and meat, and produces milk and cheese from a small dairy herd. All of these products, plus their own baked goods are sold in a farm store on site.

Volunteers are required to live and work as co-workers within the community, working shoulder-to-shoulder with mentally handicapped adults. Work takes place on the farm, in the bakery, store, coffee shop and orchards, in the administrative office and in expanded-family homes. Some 10-15 volunteers are recruited each year.

Ages 18+. No previous experience or qualifications necessary. Volunteers should have idealism, enthusiasm and an interest in personal growth.

Three months minimum

Board and lodging provided in a village home. In the first 3 months volunteers receive $50 per month pocket money, after which they may choose to join the community's system of spending flexibly according to one's own perceived needs and those of others in the community. Health insurance provided after 6 months, but not travel costs. Advice given on obtaining sponsorship.

Orientation course and newcomers' support group available during placement

Recruitment all year; apply at least six weeks in advance

Information leaflets and brochures; *Village Life* publication

CAMPHILL VILLAGE TRUST

The Secretary, Camphill Village Trust, Delrow House, Hilfield Lane, Aldenham, Watford, Hertfordshire WD2 8DJ

Watford (0923) 856006

Throughout the UK

A charity founded in 1955 which aims to provide a new and constructive way of life for mentally handicapped adults, assisting them to individual independence and social adjustment within the communities of the Trust. It guides them towards open employment while helping them to achieve full integration within society as a whole, by providing a home, work, further education and general care. The centres are based on Rudolf Steiner principles.

Volunteers are needed to work alongside the residents in every aspect of communal life at centres where the handicapped can establish themselves, work and lead a normal family life in a social background. There are three villages offering employment, two town houses for those in open employment, a college, and centres for agriculture, horticulture and assessment. Volunteers work in gardens and farms run on organic principles, craft workshops, bakeries, laundries, printing presses, and participate in the general life and chores of the community. Special emphasis is placed on social, cultural and recreational life.

Ages 20+. Applicants should have an interest and understanding in work with the mentally handicapped and be prepared to live in the same manner as the residents. Experience not essential, but an advantage. All nationalities considered. Good command of English necessary.

One year minimum, if possible

Board, lodging, and a small amount of pocket money provided; 1 day off per week

Recruitment all year

Annual Report; CVT News regular magazine; information booklet

CAMPHILL VILLAGE USA INC

Associate Director, Camphill Village USA Inc, Copake, New York 12516, United States

(518) 329 4851

New York State, United States

An international community of 220 people, about half of whom are adults with mental disabilities. Situated in 630 acres of wooded hills and farmland 110 miles north of New York City, the Village includes a farm, a large garden, 7 craft workshops, a store and 17 houses shared by 4-8 adults with disabilities and 2-4 co-workers.

Volunteers are required to live and work as co-workers within the community, taking part in work on the land, household chores, crafts, worship and cultural activities. 15-20 volunteers are recruited each year.

Ages 18+. No previous experience or qualifications necessary. Volunteers should have an open mind and a willingness to join in and experience community life. PH depending on extent of disability.

Six months minimum

Co-workers are provided with board and lodging in a village house, plus $50 per month pocket money. Those staying 12 months receive $400 towards a 3 week vacation. Health insurance provided, but not travel costs.

5-8 hours per week orientation course provided

Recruitment all year, although to participate in training programme, volunteers should plan to join in mid September

Information leaflets and booklets; *Village View* newsletter

C A R E F O R C E

Careforce, 130 City Road, London EC1V 2NJ

071-782 0013

Throughout the UK and Irish Republic

Careforce is sponsored by the Church Pastoral Aid Society, Crusaders, Scripture Union and the Universities and Colleges Christian Fellowship. It exists primarily to serve Evangelical churches and Christian organisations throughout Britain and Ireland by placing young volunteers in situations where practical help is most needed.

Volunteers work in evangelical churches, mainly in the inner-city, or with evangelical Christian organisations caring for people in need. The range of work includes clerical; cooking and cleaning; maintenance, painting and decorating; visiting, outreach and evangelism; youth and community work; and caring for the disabled or homeless. Recruits approx 90 volunteers per year.

Ages 18-23. UK and Irish Republic residents only. Applicants should be mature, committed Christians, willing to be placed where they are most needed, to serve and to learn. No previous experience or qualifications necessary.

10-12 months, beginning September

Volunteers work approx 40 hours per week. Full board and lodging with a family, in a flat or residential home provided, plus insurance cover and travel costs at beginning and end of placement. Volunteers receive £20 per week pocket money.

Compulsory 2 day course organised during first month of placement and halfway through the year

Apply October-July

Information leaflets

CENTRO LAICI ITALIANI PER LE MISSIONI

The Director, Centro Laici Italiani per le Missioni, piazza Fontana 2, 20122 Milan, Italy

Milan (02) 5839 1389   Fax (02) 5839 1390

Africa: Central African Republic, Côte d'Ivoire, Zambia

A Christian voluntary organisation founded in 1954, particularly interested in being a service to families who believe in the evangelical message. CELIM firmly believes that the Church's work does not simply revolve around the community; their main objective is the development of the Third World through professional training and agricultural advancement, and lay volunteers are recruited and prepared for work on development projects.

A limited number of volunteers are needed to work as doctors, surgeons, hospital attendants, nurses, teachers, agronomists and engineers. Projects include a Zambesi training farm pilot scheme where volunteers pass on their technical and agricultural skills, local women are taught dressmaking and cookery and a pharmacy is administered; and the development of the health and social sphere in the Central African Republic through hospital administration, training of local para-medical staff, hygiene and sanitary education, formation of local health care teams and the initiation of cooperative schemes to provide needs such as drinking water.

Ages 18+. Qualifications essential; experience useful. Knowledge of English and/or French required. Applicants should be able to give a Christian testimony during their service, and have the capacity to develop relationships with the local population. They should be able to overcome situations that are often difficult.

Two years minimum

Volunteers live in small, self-sufficient groups in houses. Pocket money, travel and insurance provided for Italian nationals only.

Orientation course arranged, about one year before departure, with the chance to discuss the work of the organisation and its programmes with returned volunteers. Special courses arranged if necessary. Advice and publications to returning volunteers.

Recruitment all year

Ad Lucem bi-monthly review; information leaflets and publications on Third World problems and international volunteering

CENTRO STUDI TERZO MONDO

The Director, Centro Studi Terzo Mondo, Via G B Morgagni 29, 20129 Milan, Italy

Milan (02) 2940 9041   Fax Milan (02) 2940 9041

Africa: Angola, Chad, Ethiopia, Mozambique, Somalia
Asia: India, Indonesia
Latin America: Brazil, Ecuador, Peru

Founded in 1962, the Centre has a wide-ranging involvement with the Third World, which includes arranging development projects, organising courses, initiating studies and research, and issuing documentation, books and journals. Also recruits volunteers for other Italian organisations employing volunteers overseas.

Volunteers are needed to work as teachers, in the medical and social services, in community work, and to organise integrated projects. Recruits 25 volunteers annually.

Ages 18+. Applicants should be reliable and have a serious commitment to voluntary work. Qualifications not always necessary but often desirable, depending on the post. All nationalities considered.

Open ended commitment

Board and accommodation depends on the country, but usually provided in private house. $100 per week pocket money and insurance provided. 36 hour week. Travel costs are met for periods of at least 6 months service. Advice given to participants on obtaining sponsorship.

Compulsory orientation course organised for those without qualifications and experience. On return, advice/debriefing meetings organised every two months.

Recruitment all year

Terzo Mondo quarterly journal; *Quaderni di Terzo Mondo* occasional publication

CHRISTIAN FOUNDATION FOR CHILDREN AND AGING

The Director of Voluntary Service, Christian Foundation for Children and Aging, One Elmwood Avenue, Kansas City, Kansas 66103

(913) 384 6500

Africa: Kenya, Madagascar.   Asia: India, Philippines.   Caribbean: Haiti, St Kitts. Latin America: Bolivia, Brazil, Chile, Colombia, Costa Rica, Dominican Republic, El Salvador, Guatemala, Honduras, Mexico, Nicaragua, Peru, Venezuela.   United States.

Founded in 1981 by former missionaries and lay volunteers, CFCA is a non-profitmaking, interdenominational organisation dedicated to help overcome hunger, disease, loneliness and suffering by caring for homeless, orphaned, crippled and abandoned children, refugees and the aged. It provides food, shelter, clothing, medicine, education, vocational and nutritional training, and pastoral and social service regardless of age, race or creed.

Volunteers needed include childcare centre workers, health care instructors, nutritionists, nurses, social/community workers, agriculturists, craft workers, teachers, recreation organisers, house parents and group home staff. Recruits approx 100 volunteers annually.

Ages 21+. Applicants should be motivated by gospel values and a Christian love which calls them to serve the poor, recognising their dignity and working with them towards self-sufficiency. Some professional skills preferred, although direct experience not necessary. Spanish/Portuguese language skills required for Latin American placements. As part of the screening process, candidates are invited to Kansas City for a discernment period; this is an opportunity for CFCA and the volunteer to find out more about each other before a commitment is made.

One year or more. Summer programme available in Venezuela.

Board and lodging provided on site by the host missionary or volunteer. Travel, insurance and pocket money provided by volunteer.

Orientation provided on mission site. CFCA stays in contact with volunteers through the laity and the religious who coordinate the child/aging sponsorship programme overseas.

Recruitment all year

Information leaflets; newsletters

CHRISTIAN OUTREACH

The Personnel Officer, Christian Outreach, 1 New Street, Leamington Spa, Warwickshire CV31 1HP

Leamington Spa (0926) 315301

Sudan, Thailand, Cambodia

Founded in 1966, Christian Outreach is a voluntary agency providing relief and development opportunities to disadvantaged children and refugees through the provision of primary health care and other facilities.

Skilled volunteers are required to provide health care in children's homes, refugee camps and rural health projects; or to assist with administration, construction projects or community development. Nurses, midwives, nutritionists, engineers, sanitation experts, builders, electricians, mechanics and community development workers are needed. Recruits 20-25 volunteers annually.

Ages 22+. Applicants should have Christian commitment, adaptability and a desire to help others. Relevant qualifications required, plus work experience in a related field. Some positions also require previous overseas experience. All nationalities considered., but recruitment is done in the UK and a good command of English is necessary.

One year contract, renewable

Volunteers are housed in local accommodation, with meals prepared by staff and approx £50 pocket money per month paid in local currency. Medical insurance, holiday allowance and travel costs provided.

Compulsory orientation course arranged; verbal debriefing and courses for returned volunteers

Recruitment all year

Prayer Letter quarterly newsletter

CHRISTIANS ABROAD

Secretary for Recruitment, Christians Abroad, 1 Stockwell Green, London SW9 9HP

071-737 7811

Mainly in Africa, the Caribbean and the Far East

An ecumenical body founded in 1972 and supported by aid and mission agencies. Provides an information and advice service on work abroad to help volunteers discover how their skills can be used and which organisations can be approached; see Advisory Bodies section. The recruitment service is provided for overseas projects seeking personnel.

Volunteers are recruited primarily to work as teachers, both primary and secondary, the greatest demand being in maths, English and sciences. EFL teachers, medical and other development specialists are also occasionally recruited.

Requirements vary according to demands of overseas organisation. Ages usually 21+. Applicants must be suitably qualified and experienced, with a wish to learn as well as to give. They should have a willingness to adjust what they know to new situations, an ability to cope with loneliness and frustration and to respect the expectations of people overseas. Qualifications and experience are more important than age.

Mainly 2 years; varies according to employer.

Terms of service vary; accommodation usually provided; local salary paid. Some posts are paid on local terms, some carry inducement allowances paid in the UK. Travel provided.

All candidates are obliged to participate in a preparation conference prior to departure, to undergo medical examination and any other training thought appropriate. A Back to Britain day is available to those returning from overseas.

Recruitment all year

See *Advisory Bodies* section for details of publications

CHURCH   MISSIONARY   SOCIETY

Experience Programmes Adviser, Church Missionary Society, 157 Waterloo Road, London SE1 8UU

071-928 8681

Africa, Asia, Middle East

Founded in 1799 in response to Christ's command to proclaim the Good News, CMS is a voluntary society set within the worldwide Anglican Communion, which sees its role as a source of interchange, not only of people with varied skills, experiences and spiritual gifts, but also of material resources, ideas, news and mutual prayer support.

Opportunities are available for volunteers to gain a cross-cultural experience of mission. Approx 15 volunteers are recruited each year.

Ages 21+. British residents only. Professional qualifications, skills, training and/or experience are required, which can be matched with specific openings in the host country. Applicants should have a positive, growing Christian faith and a desire to share this with others while working in partnership with an overseas church. They should be flexible, willing to work with others and able to live with frustrations and disappointments.

6-18 months, usually departing in September or January

Accommodation is provided by the host. All other costs need to be covered by the participant or CMS; this often includes an allowance equivalent to that of a similarly qualified national or missionary. In certain locations the volunteer receives board and lodging plus pocket money. Return air fare, medical insurance and National Insurance contributions are provided.

Compulsory 2 week training course at a missionary training college provided. Individual debriefing and corporate reorientation weekend arranged on return.

Recruitment all year

Information leaflets

COMMUNITY FOR CREATIVE NON-VIOLENCE

Intern Coordinator, Community for Creative Non-Violence, 425 2nd Street NW, Washington, DC 20001, United States

(202) 393 1909

United States: Washington, DC

CCNV has worked with Washington DC's homeless since 1971 and provides food, clothing, shelter, medical care and other services to some 2000 people each day. It aims to provide a service to the poor whilst strongly advocating an end to policies that create poverty. CCNV has a spiritual foundation expressed in many ways: whilst predominantly Christian, its religious make-up is very varied, with volunteers drawn from an assortment of backgrounds.

Volunteers are required to assist in the running of a 1400 bed shelter that includes a medical clinic, infirmary, drugs and alcohol programme, social services, outreach, central kitchen, jobs programme, library, arts and education centre. Volunteers spend four weeks working in each area of the shelter for three days; they are then placed where they are needed, with emphasis on where they prefer to work.

Ages 18+. No special skills or experience are required, but volunteers must have a sincere desire to address the issues of poverty and homelessness in a concrete, hands-on way and in an extremely diverse environment. All nationalities welcome; good knowledge of English essential.

Six months minimum

Full board dormitory accommodation provided, but no fares or wages paid. Volunteers are responsible for arranging their own US visa.

COMMUNITY SERVICE VOLUNTEERS

Volunteer Programme, Community Service Volunteers, 237 Pentonville Road, London N1 9NJ

071-278 6601

Throughout the UK

A national volunteer agency inviting all young people to experience the challenge, excitement and reward of helping people in need. For over 30 years CSV has seen the unique contribution that volunteers make to the lives of those they help.

Over 2,500 volunteers are placed each year in some 700 projects throughout the UK. Volunteers are placed according to their interests, personality, experience and the needs of the project; work is usually with individuals or small groups, not in large institutions. Project examples include independent living projects which enable individuals or families with personal difficulties or disabilities to live in their own home; volunteers help them with domestic chores and personal care, and may accompany them to work or college, or to restaurants or cinemas. Volunteers also work in group homes for people who may have a learning difficulty, who are leaving care, or who are recovering from mental illness. Volunteers help residents to lead their own lives as fully as possible by helping them with personal care and to shop, plan meals and enjoy leisure and social activities. Some placements are in hostels for homeless young people; volunteers help with administrative tasks and housework, and spend time befriending residents, talking and listening to them and helping them to find accommodation and employment or claim benefits.

Ages 16-35. Applicants should have enthusiasm, energy and a commitment to helping others in the community. No academic qualifications or previous experience necessary. B D PH W

4-12 months

Volunteers are placed away from their home area. Full board, accommodation and £21 weekly allowance provided. 40 hour week. Overseas volunteers pay £440 placement fee.

Each placement is reviewed after 1 month, and CSV staff liaise with the volunteer and project organiser throughout the placement. One person on every project is assigned to the volunteer for support and regular supervision.

Recruitment all year; placements take 6-8 weeks to arrange

Annual Review; various information leaflets, brochures and newsletters

CONCERN

CONCERN WORLDWIDE

Concern Worldwide, 248-250 Lavender Hill, Clapham Junction, London SW1W 1LJ

071-738 1033

Concern Worldwide, 47 Frederick Street, Belfast BT1 2LW

Belfast (0232) 231056

Concern, 1 Upper Camden Street, Dublin 2, Ireland

Dublin (01) 681 237/751462

Africa: Ethiopia, Mozambique, Somalia, Sudan, Tanzania, Uganda
Asia: Bangladesh, Cambodia, Laos, Thailand

A non-denominational voluntary organisation dedicated to the relief, assistance and advancement of people in the least developed countries of the world. Established in 1968 as a response by ordinary people to the tragedy of the Biafran famine, Concern and Concern Worldwide have since responded to both emergency and non-emergency situations in various African and Asian countries. Priority countries came to be chosen on the basis of their need for Concern Worldwide's services. This is often in the context of responding initially to an emergency situation, after which Concern may stay on to run welfare and basic development programmes in partnership with local organisations. Concern's income derives from public donations in the UK and Ireland, and from co-funding agencies such as the UN, the British and Irish Governments, the EC, official aid agencies and voluntary agencies.

The principal types of projects include agriculture, forestry and horticulture; preventative health care and nutrition; women's development programmes; water supply and sanitation programmes; constructing roads, bridges, schools, health clinics, other public buildings and low-cost housing; providing emergency relief in cases of natural and man-made disasters; and providing education and training through schools and literacy/numeracy programmes. Volunteers work hand in hand with local staff, assisting in the sharing of knowledge and skills throughout the community.

Ages 21+. Volunteers must be in good health and, in order to be granted an entry visa into the countries in which Concern Worldwide operates, they must hold a relevant third level qualification. They should have good communication skills, be adaptable and sensitive to cultures different from their own.

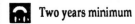 Two years minimum

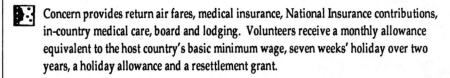 Concern provides return air fares, medical insurance, National Insurance contributions, in-country medical care, board and lodging. Volunteers receive a monthly allowance equivalent to the host country's basic minimum wage, seven weeks' holiday over two years, a holiday allowance and a resettlement grant.

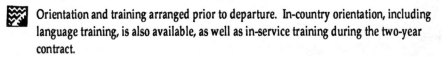 Orientation and training arranged prior to departure. In-country orientation, including language training, is also available, as well as in-service training during the two-year contract.

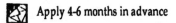 Apply 4-6 months in advance

CORRYMEELA COMMUNITY

Volunteer Coordinator, The Corrymeela Community, Ballycastle, Co Antrim, BT54 6QU

Ballycastle (026 57) 62626

Northern Ireland

Founded in 1965, Corrymeela is situated on the north Antrim coast, and comprises a house, cottages and youth village, supported by the Corrymeela Community, a group drawn from many different Christian traditions who work for reconciliation in Northern Ireland in conflict situations and promote a concern for issues of peace and justice in the wider world. People under stress, such as those from problem areas, families of prisoners, the disabled and many others, go to Corrymeela for a break or holiday; conferences and other activities challenge participants to look critically at contemporary issues.

A limited number of volunteers are needed to participate in the programme work of the residential centre, working with the groups who use the centre and being the link during their stay. They should expect to be involved in the practical aspects of running the establishment, assisting with catering arrangements, preparing accommodation, and working in the kitchen, laundry or reception. Usually 10 long-term volunteers are recruited each year, 5 from Ireland, 5 from overseas.

Ages 18-30. Some experience of community life and working with people helpful but not essential. Applicants must be fit and adaptable to cope with the demands and pressures of community life and a very busy programme; open to people of all ages, backgrounds and traditions; good at communicating with others; with a commitment to the process of reconciliation. All nationalities considered; good command of English essential.

One or two years, starting September. Also limited number of 3-6 month placements available starting after Christmas, plus short-term summer opportunities.

Accommodation in twin bedrooms with all meals, £20 per week pocket money and medical/dental cover provided. Each volunteer receives an agreed sum to help pay for travel home. 6 days free per month; 1 week's holiday for every 3 months service.

Prospective volunteers are asked to spend a few days at Corrymeela before applying. One week induction period after acceptance. Weekly briefing and reflection programme with the full-time volunteer coordinator. Great care is taken in terms of staff support, external consultancy and pastoral access.

Apply December-February; interviews held in April

DIENST OVER GRENZEN

The Secretariat, Dienst Over Grenzen, PO Box 177, 3700 AD Zeist, The Netherlands

Zeist (03404) 24884

Mainly in Africa, with limited opportunities in Asia and Latin America

Founded in 1962, a personnel recruiting agency serving as a mediator rather than employer, working on behalf of churches, church-related organisations and governments in the Third World. When DOG receives a request for personnel, a decision whether to recruit is taken within the framework of DOG's own policies and priorities. An insight into whether the project concerned contributes to the improvement of the socio-economic situation of underprivileged groups in the developing countries and as to the precise task of the development workers within these projects is involved. DOG keeps a register of volunteers qualified in different professions and the agencies abroad can submit requests for personnel.

There are vacancies in the medical, technical, educational, administration, financial and community development fields. Personnel required include doctors, nurses, physiotherapists and analysts; construction, mechanical and agricultural engineers; teachers in science, agriculture, mechanics, technical and vocational subjects; and social workers.

Ages 25+. Dutch nationals only. Volunteers should be qualified to MSc/BSc degree level or equivalent. Previous experience an advantage.

Three years minimum

There are no set rules for salaries and allowances. The local salary should cover living expenses, housing, insurance and, if possible, travel costs. Interview expenses not provided.

Compulsory orientation course arranged by a joint institute of the Protestant Missions in the Netherlands. Additional training such as language or professional courses can also be arranged. Advice and debriefing provided on return if necessary.

Recruitment all year

Doggersbank quarterly communication bulletin, published in Dutch; information leaflet

E A S T   E U R O P E A N   P A R T N E R S H I P

Programme Officer, East European Partnership, 15 Princeton Court, 53-55 Felsham Road, London SW15 1AZ

081-780 2841

Eastern Europe: Albania, Bulgaria, Czechlands/Slovakia, Hungary, Poland and Romania

An initiative set up in 1990 by VSO. It posts skilled men and women abroad in response to requests from east European countries, where the process of reconstruction is taking place in the face of enormous political, social and economic difficulties. Volunteers share their skills with local colleagues in an effort to help re-establish the self-sufficiency of the host country. It is hoped that after several years the skills which EEP has been asked to supply will be locally available, and a volunteer programme will no longer be required.

Includes humanities teaching and English teaching (EFL and ESP) in schools and colleges; nursery nurses, paediatric and sick children's nurses and mental handicap nurses to work as in-service trainers in children's homes, as well as social workers with experience of residential childcare and fostering, in Romania; also mental handicap nurses, special needs teachers and social workers with experience in mental handicap to work in Albania.

Ages 22-70. Volunteers must have English to mother tongue standard, appropriate qualifications and significant full-time work experience. English language teaching posts require graduates with a TEFL qualification; childcare qualifications include NNEB, SCOTVEC, City and Guilds in Childcare and the Certificate of Hospital Play Specialists; social workers should hold the CQSW. Applicants should have a genuine desire to assist in the long-term development of the countries of Eastern Europe. They should be in good health, adaptable, tolerant, resilient in the face of frustrations and able to cope with difficult working and living conditions. **B D PH W**

Two years for teaching posts; 1 year for childcare/social work in Romania and Albania

The overseas employer provides a salary based on local equivalent (typically £50-£100 per month), accommodation, free medical services and concessions on internal travel and accommodation. EEP provides return travel expenses, training, medical/dental treatment not covered by employer, equipment grant, mid-tour grant and resettlement grant, NI contributions, visa fees and accident insurance.

Compulsory 10-14 day pre-departure training provided. Debriefing and advice on resettlement provided on return.

Most postings in September or January. Apply at least 3 months in advance.

Link newsletter

EDINBURGH CYRENIANS

The Coordinator, Edinburgh Cyrenians, 20 Broughton Place, Edinburgh EH1 3RX

031-556 4971

Edinburgh and West Lothian

Set up in June 1968 to develop and provide services to homeless single people, the Edinburgh Cyrenian Trust runs a city community in central Edinburgh and a rural project on a small organic farm in West Lothian. Residents are a mix of young people referred by social workers, hospitals or other agencies.

Volunteers are required to live and work alongside residents and other volunteers, sharing the jobs involved in running a large household, with particular responsibility for managing household accounts, upholding the rules of the community, attending weekly meetings, forming helpful relationships with community members and offering assistance and support to residents. Community life is challenging, difficult and stressful, but can also be extremely rewarding. Some 22 volunteers are recruited annually.

Ages 18-30. Applicants should have personal commitment, open-mindedness, willingness to learn, a sense of responsibility, energy, enthusiasm and a sense of humour.
No previous experience or qualifications. All nationalities accepted; working knowledge of English essential. B D PH unsuitable for wheelchairs.

6+ months

Volunteers work a 5 day week and receive full board accommodation in the community, with access to a flat away from the community on days off. £24 per week pocket money provided, plus £160 grant for 1 week's holiday after 3 months, £30 clothing allowance and £135 leaving grant after 6 months.

Regular training is given and volunteers are supervised by non-residential social workers

Recruitment all year

Annual Report; information pack.

FÖRENINGEN
STAFFANSGÅRDEN

The Director, Föreningen Staffansgården, Box 66, Furugatan 1, 82060 Delsbo, Sweden

0653-16850

Delsbo, Sweden

A Camphill village consisting of a training school for adolescents with mental handicaps and a nearby farm for handicapped adults. The community also has a garden, a bakery, eight family houses, and workshops for weaving and woodwork.

Co-workers are required to live and work with mentally handicapped people, playing a full part in village life including domestic tasks, crafts and farmwork.

Ages 19+. No previous experience or qualifications necessary, but applicants must have a strong desire to share a period of their life with handicapped people. Applicants should be willing to learn Swedish; courses are provided. B D PH

Six months minimum; 1 year preferred.

Co-workers receive board and lodging in a village home shared with 10-15 other people, plus pocket money to cover their immediate needs. Accident and health insurance provided. Ticket home paid after 6 month stay.

Training seminars and courses organised in arts, therapy and the philosophy of anthroposophy

Recruitment all year

FRONTIERS FOUNDATION / OPERATION BEAVER

The Program Coordinator, Frontiers Foundation/Operation Beaver, 2615 Danforth Avenue, Suite 203, Toronto, Ontario, M4C 1L6, Canada

Toronto (416) 690 3930

Alberta, Ontario and Northwest Territories, Canada

Works in cooperation with requesting communities to fulfil basic housing needs. Volunteers from all over the world make practical efforts in reducing poverty, do volunteer work, and meet people from culturally diverse backgrounds. Also run recreation programmes providing stimulating and creative alternatives to the boredom and social problems endemic in many Native American communities.

About 80% of volunteers work on practical projects in cooperation with Native and non-Native peoples in rural communities in Ontario, Alberta and Northwest Territories. Construction projects involve building or renovating wood frame or log houses. Recreation volunteers work in Alberta with local youth workers organising games, camp-outs and other activities for the youth of the community during the summer months.

Ages 18+. Older applicants must feel competent to perform manual labour. Applicants should be hardworking, open-minded, flexible and culturally sensitive. They must also be able to live without luxuries like television, flush toilets, and in some cases without running water or electricity. Volunteers with construction skills are given first priority, and previous voluntary experience is also an asset. For recreation projects applicants should have experience of working on camps or with children.

12+ weeks (16+ weeks for Northwest Territories), beginning April-October; most volunteers arrive for the summer session, June-August. Service can be extended for up to 18 months, depending on performance in first period.

Salary not provided, although a modest living allowance is paid after 12 week minimum period. Accommodation, food, local travel expenses and insurance provided. Travel to Canada and to the orientation site (Toronto or Edmonton) is the volunteer's responsibility.

Volunteers receive detailed information in the application kit. Intensive 2 day orientation for summer session volunteers; others participate in a less formal 1 day orientation.

At least 3 months in advance; recruitment all year

GERMAN LEPROSY RELIEF ASSOCIATION

The Personnel Manager, Germany Leprosy Relief Association, Deutsches Aussätzigen-Hilfswerk eV, Dominikanerplatz 4, Postfach 11 04 62, 8700 Wurzburg 11, Germany

Wurzburg (0931) 50784

Africa: Egypt, Ethiopia, Senegal, Sierra Leone, Tanzania, Togo, Uganda
Latin America: Bolivia, Brazil, Colombia, Paraguay

Founded in 1957 with the tasks of sponsoring and establishing institutions to combat leprosy; training, education and other means of rehabilitation for leprosy patients; public health education and publicity. The declared aim of the association is to integrate leprosy control services into general health care programmes wherever possible, as well as supporting public health care work and the training of local personnel for the medical and social welfare sector.

There are vacancies for skilled long-term volunteers, helping at treatment and training centres, on national health care and control programmes, and in the general care of leprosy patients.

Ages 25+. Applicants must have a commitment to the care of leprosy patients. Academic qualifications required, plus several years of skilled, professional experience. All nationalities considered. Knowledge of English, Spanish and French required, depending on the host country.

Three years

Accommodation in house or apartment, monthly allowance depending on marital status, insurance and travel costs provided. 40-50 hour week.

Compulsory orientation course arranged

Recruitment all year

Information leaflets; several publications in the German language

GIRL GUIDES ASSOCIATION (UK)

The International Secretary, Girl Guides Association, 17-19 Buckingham Palace Road, London SW1W 0PT

071-834 6242

India, Mexico, Switzerland, London

The Girl Guides Association of the United Kingdom, founded in 1920 by Robert Baden Powell, is a voluntary organisation for girls. It gives them the opportunity to follow any number of interests and at the same time learn self-reliance and self respect. Guides share a commitment to a common standard set out in the Promise and Law.

Volunteer work is available in London and overseas at centres owned by the World Association of Girl Guides and Girl Scouts. Projects may include assisting the development of Guide Associations, training adult leaders or administration duties in connection with Guide House. The work is sometimes strenuous and the hours long.

Ages 18+. Qualifications and experience required vary according to the position. Volunteers must be members of the Association. B D PH considered.

Duration variable

Board, accommodation and pocket money provision vary according to the position. Insurance provided in some cases. Travel costs usually paid by the volunteer. Advice is given to participants on obtaining sponsorship. Members are encouraged to write articles for the magazines on their return.

Recruitment all year

The Brownie; Today's Guide; Guiding magazines

GLASGOW SIMON COMMUNITY

Depute Manager, Glasgow Simon Community, Flat 0/2, 40 Westmoreland Street, Govanhill, Glasgow, G42

Glasgow, Scotland

Aims to offer time, friendship, practical help and supportive accommodation to men and women who have been homeless for some time.

Volunteers work in 4 small group homes where residents and volunteers live together, sharing in the running and day-to-day life. Contact is made with homeless people, especially rough sleepers, and friendship and practical help are offered. 12 volunteers work on the projects, for a minimum of 6 months.

Ages 18+. No academic qualifications required. Previous experience or work with homeless people is an advantage, but not essential. Volunteers should have a non-patronising, non-judgmental attitude towards homelessness and drug/alcohol addiction and the ability to accept people for what they are and cope with stress and emotional pressures.

6+ months

Five day week, 24 hour day. Volunteers receive £15.70 per week plus £21.61 per week compulsory savings which is paid in lump sum at end of placement. £40 shoe allowance per year. £79.75 for 10 day holiday every 3 months. Full board accommodation provided with separate accommodation for days off. Travel costs paid up to £50 maximum return fare.

Three week induction course, plus informal one-to-one training during the first month, with training visits to relevant agencies. Regular opportunities to participate in training events and attend conferences.

Recruitment all year; apply 3-6 months in advance

Learning to Care; Simon News; Annual Report

GREAT GEORGES PROJECT

The Duty Officer, Great Georges Project, The Blackie, Great George Street, Liverpool 1

051-709 5109

Liverpool

Founded in 1968, the Great Georges Community Cultural Project, known locally as The Blackie, is a centre for experimental work in the arts, sports, games and education of today. It is housed in a former church in an area typical of the modern inner-city - multi-racial, relatively poor, with a high crime rate and a high energy level - sometimes a lot of fun. The project sets about its task of building bridges between the artist and the community with great enthusiasm, offering a wide range of cultural programmes, workshops and exhibitions, including pottery, sculpture, printing, film/video making, photography, painting, writing, outdoor plays, carpentry, puppetry, playstructures, music, mime and dance. Open 7 days a week, 10.00-24.00.

Volunteers are needed to work with children/adults in projects undertaken at the Project and in the local community, with endless opportunities to learn and create. The general work of running the Project is shared as much as possible, with everyone doing some administration, cleaning, talking to visitors and playing games with the children. Recruits 100-150 volunteers annually.

Ages 18+. Applicants should have a good sense of humour, stamina, a readiness to learn, and a willingness to work hard and share any skills they may have. The children/young people who visit the Project are tough, intelligent, friendly and regard newcomers as a fair target for jokes, so the ability to exert discipline without being authoritarian is essential. No direct experience required. All nationalities considered. Good working knowledge of English needed.

1+ months. Volunteers are particularly needed at Christmas, Easter and summer.

Accommodation in shared rooms at staff house; long-term volunteers may have own room. Vegetarian breakfast and evening meal provided; cooking on a rota basis. Those who can afford to, contribute approx £15 per week to cover food and housekeeping. Wages generally paid after 6 months. 12 hour day minimum, 6 day week.

Orientation course includes a talk with films and a pack of Project literature

Recruitment all year

HABITAT FOR HUMANITY
INTERNATIONAL INC

The Volunteer Coordinator, Habitat for Humanity International Inc, 121 Habitat Street, Americus, Georgia 31709, United States

(912) 924 6935

Thirty four developing countries worldwide, and over 700 affiliates in the United States

An ecumenical Christian housing ministry which seeks to eliminate poverty housing from the world and make decent shelter a matter of conscience and action. Builds low-cost homes for sale to poor families at no profit and no interest, each homeowner investing work-hours into the construction of their home. Both needy and affluent people work together in equal partnership, forging new relationships and a sense of community.

Volunteers are required to take on the role of International Partners, working in partnership with local community leaders, assisting the local construction programme. The IPs' ultimate goal is to work themselves out of a job by enabling their national partners to assume the administration of the project.

Ages 21+. Applicants must have experience in administration, construction, management or community organising, with good communications skills, experience of working with committees and an ability to relate well to people of various backgrounds. Previous work with Habitat in the United States useful. Habitat is a Christian organisation making no demands on denominational affiliation, but applicants should have a faith commitment and be motivated by a desire to make a difference in the housing situation worldwide.

Three years for International Partners; 3 months minimum for other work in the US

Housing, health insurance, vacation time and a stipend provided, and some international travel costs are covered. To keep costs to a minimum volunteers are asked to raise as much financial support as they can before they go.

International Partners undergo training at Habitat's headquarters, covering topics such as Habitat's philosophy, intercultural awareness, community organising and development issues, project management and appropriate construction techniques. There are also retreats organised while in the field, plus re-entry classes and a resettlement allowance.

Recruitment all year; apply 6-12 months in advance for international service, or 2-3 months in advance for service in the United States.

Information leaflets; *Habitat World* bi-monthly newsletter; *Sharing Habitat* catalogue listing books, slide shows, video and audio cassettes, and films.

HOMES FOR HOMELESS PEOPLE

The Volunteer Recruitment Officer, Homes for Homeless People, 90-92 Bromham Road, Bedford, MK40 2QH

Bedford (0234) 350853

Throughout the UK

Founded in 1970, a national federation of local voluntary housing projects providing support and shared housing for the single homeless, who are amongst the most vulnerable and disadvantaged people in society, and whose housing needs are largely ignored. Encourages member groups to achieve a high standard of provision for their residents, and encourages residents to participate in decision-making. Provides a public information service and a volunteer recruitment and placement service.

Volunteers are required to help operate homeless accommodation projects, living alongside and working for the benefit of homeless people. The work is challenging, rewarding and ideally suited to those aiming for a career in a caring profession. Some 30 volunteers are recruited annually.

Ages 18-35. All nationalities considered. Fluent English essential. Applicants should have honesty, self-assurance, common sense, the ability to mix with people from all walks of life, a sense of humour and a commitment to helping homeless people. Basic DIY skills and some experience of living away from home helpful.

6-12 months

Terms and conditions of work vary according to the project. Board, lodging, travel costs on joining and leaving the project and £30-£50 per week pocket money usually provided.

Briefing depends on individual project. all projects are encouraged to provide training, supervision and support There is usually a 2-week trial period for volunteers.

Recruitment all year

No Home of Their Own and *You Can't Put People in Little Boxes* information leaflets

HT SCOTLAND

The Volunteer Coordinator, HT Scotland, 4 Drum Street, Gilmerton, Edinburgh EH17 8QG

031-658 1096

Throughout Scotland and occasionally Northern Ireland

A voluntary organisation founded in 1989 to provide advice, information and support to projects using horticulture in their work with people with disabilities.

Volunteers are needed to work on horticultural projects with handicapped, disabled and disadvantaged people. Projects take place in residential, often rural settings where horticulture/gardening is used for therapy, training, rehabilitation or recreational purposes. Volunteers may work alongside a salaried horticulturist, or may be the only horticulturist on the project.

Ages 20+. Applicants must be self-confident, enthusiastic and adaptable, with plenty of initiative, openness towards disabilities and a desire to work with people from all walks of life, especially those with special needs. Qualifications, skills and/or basic experience in horticulture or gardening preferable. All nationalities considered. B D PH W

6-12 months

Volunteers work a maximum of 40 hours per week. Full board and lodging provided on or off site, plus £20 per week pocket money, insurance and initial travel expenses to project. One week's leave every four months, by arrangement with project management.

Some training given on-site, plus evaluation. At end of placement advice is given on further training opportunities and jobs in the horticultural therapy field.

Recruitment all year; apply 2-3 months in advance

Annual Review; information leaflets; occasional papers; *Growth Point* newsletter; *Gardening is for Everyone* ideas for gardening activities with handicapped people in mind; *Able to Garden* a practical guide for disabled and elderly gardeners

INDEPENDENT LIVING
SCHEMES

Kenneth Smith & Dorothy Kendrick, Independent Living Schemes, Lewisham Social Services, Laurence House, 1 Catford Road, London SE6 4SW

081-695 6000 exts 8639/8638

Lewisham, south east London

Aims to enable severely disabled people (all wheelchair users) to lead the lifestyle of their choice, living in their own homes rather than in hospitals or residential care.

Volunteer helpers carry out everyday tasks for the disabled person such as cooking, housework and shopping; assist with personal care including toiletting, bathing and lifting; and share social, community and leisure activities.

Ages 18-50. No experience necessary, just commonsense and a caring attitude.
B D PH considered, depending on ability.

Six months minimum preferred

Rent-free accommodation sharing with other helpers is provided near to the scheme. Household bills are met and volunteers receive a weekly allowance of £20 pocket money and £30 for food. In addition, £12 per month is provided for clothing and leisure. Travel expenses paid within the UK at beginning and end of placement. 1 week's paid leave after 4 months.

Training given on project. Supervision and advice available from ILS team social worker and administrative worker.

Recruitment all year. Write or telephone for application form and information pack.

I N N I S F R E E   V I L L A G E

The Volunteer Coordinator, Innisfree Village, Route 2, Box 506, Crozet, Virginia 22932, United States

(804) 823 5400   Fax (804) 823 5027

United States

Innisfree's goal is to provide a lifetime residential facility for adults with mental disabilities. The staff consists of volunteers who life and work together with mentally disabled co-workers in a natural and humanistic environment.

Acting as houseparents and co-workers, volunteers are needed to work on the 600 acre farm in the foothills of the Blue Ridge Mountains with the choice of working in the bakery, weavery, woodshop, garden or free school. Recruits 18-20 volunteers annually.

Ages 21+. Volunteers need energy, enthusiasm, patience, and a willingness to work with the 'differently abled'. They must be in excellent health, and interested in the community process in a very rural setting. Volunteers must be college graduates or equivalent, preferably with some experience of working with mentally disabled, recently brain injured or emotionally ill people. Craft skills greatly appreciated. All nationalities considered. Fluent English required.

Volunteers are sponsored under the International Exchange Visitors Programme for 1 year minimum, and have J-1 Visa status

Volunteers have their own room and board in a house of 6-14 people. $150 per month spending money, $100 Christmas bonus, medical insurance and up to $250 for dental expenses provided. Travel costs are paid by volunteer. Volunteers work a 5 day week, with 2 consecutive days free. Annual holiday entitlement of 21 days, with an additional holiday allowance of $30 per day. In addition, severance pay is accrued at $45 per month.

The first month is a mandatory trial period with four orientation sessions covering a brief history of the village and its guidelines, and volunteers are encouraged to get to know the village as well as possible before settling down in one house. At the end of this period, the community evaluates and decides the best placement for the volunteer. Innisfree can provide interested applicants with the names and addresses of former volunteers from England whom they may wish to contact for further information.

Recruitment all year

INTERNATIONAL COOPERATION
FOR DEVELOPMENT

 The Recruitment Officer, International Cooperation for Development, Unit 3, Canonbury Yard, 190a New North Road, London N1 7BJ

071-354 0883

Africa: Namibia, Zimbabwe; Caribbean: Haiti; Middle East: Yemen; Latin America: Dominican Republic, Ecuador, El Salvador, Honduras, Nicaragua, Peru.

A charity receiving funds from the Overseas Development Administration, the EC, UK development agencies and private sponsors; has been recruiting experienced professionals to share their skills with communities in the Third World since 1965. Works with locally based partners, including community organisations and government ministries, who share a commitment to improving local people's lives and working for a just and equal society. Will only work on a project if there is a real need for ICD worker's skills; a strong skills transfer or training element; the poorer or less advantaged of the community are the main beneficiaries; and the role and needs of women are taken into account.

Areas of work include primary health care and health education; teacher training; food technology and nutrition; environment and public health; literacy education; agricultural training; youth skills training; engineering/mechanics; community based rehabilitation; cooperative/small business training; popular communication and community education work; computer and information technology. Majority of posts available are for health workers, agriculturalists, popular education and literacy workers.

Ages mid-20s to mid-60s. Applicants must have appropriate professional qualifications with a minimum of 2 years' work experience and preferably a background in formal or informal training. They must be keen to share their skills with communities in the Third World, self-motivated, sensitive and able to adapt their lifestyle to a new culture.

Two years minimum

Pre-departure grant, accommodation, essential household equipment, salary based on local rates, insurance and return travel provided. National Insurance contributions and home savings allowance also paid. Dependants' allowance available in some cases.

Compulsory 2 week course arranged in London, plus orientation on arrival. One-day debriefing provided on return.

Posts advertised throughout the year; monthly list available on request. Those currently unable to go overseas may register and will be informed when a suitable post arises.

Information leaflet

INTERNATIONAL HEALTH EXCHANGE

The Director, International Health Exchange, Africa Centre, 38 King Street, London WC2E 8JT

071-836 5833

Africa: Egypt, Ethiopia, Ghana, Guinea-Bissau, Kenya, Liberia, Malawi, Mozambique, Nigeria, Seychelles, Sierra Leone, Sudan, Tanzania, Transkei, Uganda, Zaire, Zambia, Zimbabwe;   Asia: Bangladesh, Bhutan, India, Maldives, Nepal, Pakistan; Caribbean: Grenada, Nevis;   Far East: Indonesia, Malaysia, Thailand; Latin America: Brazil;   Middle East: Lebanon, United Arab Emirates: Pacific: Aboriginal freehold lands of Central Australia, Fiji, Papua New Guinea, Philippines, Western Samoa.

A charity founded in 1980 as a coordinating agency for experienced health workers. It is not a recruiting agency, but runs a register for health workers interested in working in developing countries, acting as a clearing house for those planning to work overseas. Also publishes a bi-monthly magazine which, as well as carrying job and course listings, explores practical approaches to primary health care in developing countries.

Runs a register of 1000 health workers including doctors, nurses, physiotherapists, nutritionists, health administrators and health educators. Bi-monthly magazine goes to all register members and is available on subscription, lists health posts, agencies and details of training courses.

Nurses must be SRN and have at least two years' post-qualification experience; most useful areas are midwifery and community nursing. Doctors should have at least one year's post-registration experience; most useful areas are paediatrics, general practice, obstetrics and gynaecology. Other requirements depend on the recruiting agencies.

1-2 years, but occasionally there are opportunities for periods of a few months

Contractual details vary according to the recruiting agency and are outside the responsibility of IHE

Recruitment all year round

The Health Exchange bi-monthly magazine; *Annual Report*; advice sheets for doctors, nurses and health workers intending to work in developing countries

INTERSERVE

Yvonne Dorey, Personnel Director, Interserve, 325 Kennington Road, London SE11 4QH

071-735 8227

India and Pakistan

A member-society of the Evangelical Missionary Alliance, Interserve is an international evangelical mission with over 400 partners in a wide range of ministry in South Asia and the Middle East, along with several serving among Asian ethnic groups in Britain. It is voluntarily staffed by Christians from both Asia and the West.

Volunteers serve local Christian groups, teaching English, working with computers and caring for children. There are opportunities to learn about missionary work. Recruits seven volunteers per year for its school leaver's programme.

Ages 18+. UK residents only. Applicants must be committed Christians who are involved with their local church/school Christian Union. They should have a good general education to A level standard or equivalent.

7-10 months, beginning October

Volunteers work an average of 30 hours per week, and stay with Christian families or in a hostel. They are responsible for all travel and insurance costs, as well as board and lodging costs and personal expenses whilst on placement.

Compulsory orientation course provided before departure, and personal interview and follow-up at end of placement

Apply as soon as possible, as places are limited

JOINT ASSISTANCE CENTRE

The Convenor, Joint Assistance Centre, H-65, South Extension 1, New Delhi 11049, India

Throughout India

A small voluntary group for disaster assistance working in close liaison with other groups throughout India who run voluntary projects of various kinds

Operate a learn while you travel scheme whereby volunteers either do administrative work at centres in Delhi or are placed on short stay workcamps with groups in other areas to help in environmental activities, agriculture, construction, community work, health and sanitation work, teaching first aid or preparation work for disasters. Specific projects are also organised including work on playschemes, organising fundraising campaigns and exhibitions to increase awareness, and teaching English in a village school near Delhi.

Ages 18+. Experience welcome but not essential. Applicants should have a personal faith in God, and an open mind towards new beliefs. They should be adaptable to difficult situations and have patience, tolerance, understanding and organisational skills. Conditions are very primitive, and the summers (May/June) are very hot. Only vegetarian food is allowed, and applicants must comply with no alcohol/tobacco/drugs rule.

3-6 months commitment preferred

JAC believes that those fortunate enough to have the opportunities of higher education or travel abroad have benefited from the resources available in their society. Therefore each volunteer is required to make a contribution in order participate in voluntary service, usually £60 per month. Self-catering accommodation provided; volunteers share in all housekeeping duties. Registration fee £10. No travel, insurance or pocket money provided. Volunteers must make their own arrangements for obtaining a visa. Travel within India is paid only if it is on JAC business.

No prior briefing arranged, but there are opportunities to take part in disaster management programmes and conferences. Can also put applicants in touch with former volunteers.

Apply at least 3 months in advance to Friends of JAC, c/o 15 Burkes Road, Beaconsfield, Buckinghamshire HP9 1PB; enclose a cheque for £2 made out to Friends of JAC to cover postage

LALMBA ASSOCIATION

The Medical Director, Lalmba Association, 7685 Quartz Street, Golden, Colorado 80403, United States

(303) 420 1810

Africa: Kenya, Sudan, Ethiopia
Latin America: Mexico

Lalmba is the Ethiopian word for *place of hope*; the Association is a small medical relief agency which started work in Ethiopia in 1963, moving to the borders of Sudan and Ethiopia with the increase of refugees during the late 1970s. It now runs feeding centres and a food distribution programme, orphanages, medical centres, eye and prosthetics clinics, education centres, refugee camps and a development bank. Lalmba's aims are to provide primary medical care whilst teaching and training local populations to care for their own needs as much as possible.

The main requirements are for doctors, ophthalmologists, prosthestists and nurses. Physicians are responsible for teaching and supervising native community health workers, general medical practice, and providing primary health care with preventive medicine and education. Nurses have an expanded role and their work includes physical examinations, internal lab studies and diagnosis. Staff travel to the refugee camps and villages, providing medication for malnutrition and ailments such as dysentery, parasites, malaria, tuberculosis and eye diseases.

Ages 25-70. Relevant medical qualifications and experience essential. Applicants must have dedication and be committed to serving extremely poor, famine-stricken refugees. All nationalities considered. Good command of English required.

One to three years

Accommodation provided in well-appointed grass huts, with electricity and water nearby, and communal catering. All positions are non-salaried; living expenses, travel costs, health and life insurance provided. Eight hour day, five day week.

Lalmba meet and brief all volunteers personally; orientation organised in the form of videos and slides.

Recruitment all year; apply 6-12 months in advance

Newsletter; information leaflets

LAND USE VOLUNTEERS

The Volunteer Coordinator, Land Use Volunteers, Horticultural Therapy, Goulds Ground, Vallis Way, Frome, Somerset BA11 3DW

Frome (0373) 464782

England and Wales

The Society for Horticultural Therapy is a non-profitmaking company founded in 1978 to help disabled and handicapped people enjoy and benefit from gardening, horticulture and agriculture. Land Use Volunteers, its volunteer service began in 1981, is one of a wide range of practical services offered to disabled people and those who work with them.

Volunteers are needed to work with handicapped, disabled and disadvantaged people, living and working on rehabilitation projects on the basis of a common interest in plants and animals to enable land use activities work more effectively. Past projects have included developing a small hospital market garden whilst working with psychiatric patients and care staff; working with adult mentally handicapped residents at a home farm, breeding rare domestic animals and organic growing; training clients and other care staff in simple horticultural tasks; and working with ex-drug addicts and offenders in planting and gardening. Also work with the physically handicapped, the hearing impaired, the blind, the elderly and disturbed young people.

Ages 18+. Applicants must have qualifications, skills and basic experience in agriculture, horticulture, forestry or any related environmental discipline and a willingness to transmit their skills to others. They should also be self-confident, adaptable and able to fit into a small community. Experience of working with people who have disabilities an advantage. B D PH W

6-12 months

Full board and lodging provided on or off site, plus at least £20 pocket money per week and initial travel expenses to project. One week vacation every four weeks, by arrangement with project management.

Recruitment all year

Annual Review; information leaflets; occasional papers; *Growth Point* newsletter; *Gardening is for Everyone* ideas for gardening activities with handicapped people in mind; *Able to Garden* a practical guide for disabled and elderly gardeners

LANKA JATHIKA SARVODAYA SANGAMAYA (INC)

The Director, SSI, Lanka Jathika Sarvodaya Sangamaya (Inc), Damsak Mandira, 98 Rawatawatta Road, Moratuwa, Sri Lanka

(01) 507159/505255

Sri Lanka

Founded in 1958, the movement is a large, non-governmental people's self development effort covering nearly 8,000 villages. The people have provided a practical possibility of realising Mahatma Gandhi's concept of a world society where the well-being of all shall be ensured. It aims to create awareness among economically and socially deprived communities and to mobilise latent human and material potential for the satisfaction of basic human needs in a manner that ensures sustainable development.

Volunteers are needed mainly on village-level development projects in agriculture, animal husbandry, agriculture-based industry, appropriate technology, economic activities, irrigation, sanitation, house construction, energy conservation and the development of alternative energy sources. Opportunities also for teachers in pre-school and primary education, and for the provision of preventive and curative health care including nursing, nutrition, feeding programmes, health education and rehabilitation of the handicapped.

Ages 21+. A willingness to teach and to learn is the main consideration; applicants should have an awareness of their responsibility to improve human conditions wherever needed and an ability to work in sometimes difficult circumstances. They should also have a commitment to the promotion of peace and international understanding, and to an ideal that leads to the equitable distribution of the world's resources according to need. Recognised skills and experience preferred, but specialised skills are not a priority requirement, and academic qualifications are optional. All nationalities considered.

Six months minimum; visas extended at the discretion of the authorities in Sri Lanka

Board and lodging provided at a cost not exceeding Rs200 per day, but may be less in out-stations. Volunteers are expected to meet their own travel, insurance and living expenses.

Compulsory orientation organised. End of service evaluation provided, at which the volunteer's subsequent activities and placement in the home country are discussed.

Recruitment all year, depending on availability of vacancies

Various pamphlets on the work and ideals of the movement

L'ARCHE LIMITED

The General Secretary, L'Arche Limited, 14 London Road, Beccles, Suffolk NR34 9NH
from mid 1993: 10 Briggate, Silsden, Keighley, West Yorkshire BD20 9JT

Beccles (0502) 715329 *from mid 1993*: Keighley (0535) 656186

England & Wales: Bognor Regis, Brecon, Kent, Lambeth, Liverpool
Scotland: Edinburgh, Inverness
Some opportunities also exist to serve with L'Arche overseas

An international federation of communities in which handicapped people and those who help them live, work and share their lives together. Founded in 1964 in northern France, there are now some 95 communities worldwide. L'Arche believe that each person, whether handicapped or not, has a unique and mysterious value; handicapped people are complete human beings and as such have the right to life, care, education and work. They also believe that those with less capacity for autonomy are capable of great love, and are loved by God in a special way. L'Arche was founded on a deep belief in the teachings of the Gospels and the simple, spiritual life is considered very important to L'Arche Communities.

Assistants are required to share their lives with handicapped people, living and working as members of L'Arche Communities. Some 60-70 Assistants are recruited each year.

Ages 18-50. No previous experience necessary, but applicants must have a commitment to living in community and be interested in caring for disabled people. Communities are Christian based, but welcome people of all faiths, or none.

Twelve months minimum

Full board and lodging provided, plus £25+ per week pocket money and insurance (employers' liability and personal). Applicants pay their own travel and personal expenses.

All placements involve a trial period of a week or weekend, with an exit interview at the end of the placement

Apply as far in advance as possible; no deadline

UK *Newsletter; Letters of L'Arche* quarterly journal; various books, leaflets, video and audio cassettes describing the history, philosophy and life of L'Arche Communities

LATIN LINK

Squadron Leader Michael Cole OBE, Director, Short-Term Experience Projects (STEP), Latin Link, Whitefield House, 186 Kennington Park Road, London SE11 4B

071-582 4952

Argentina, Bolivia, Brazil, Nicaragua, Peru

Latin Link is a fellowship of personnel in Latin America and elsewhere, who, alongside their supporters and supporting churches, are committed to demonstrating the interdependence of the worldwide church, encouraging cross cultural mission and channelling resources to and from Latin America for the benefit of the church worldwide.

Short-Term Experience Projects provide a means of allowing people to work in partnership with the Latin American church, building and extending orphanages, churches, community centres and schools. Projects involve a wide spectrum of tasks and skills, from evangelism through the graphic arts to bricklaying and carpentry.

Ages 18-35. Older applicants with special skills welcomed. Applicants must have a Christian commitment and outlook and a willingness to work as a team with Latin Americans. No previous experience or qualifications necessary, although skills in music or drama, knowledge of Spanish or Portuguese, medical qualifications and practical skills are useful. B D PH depending on extent of handicap.

Spring teams: 4 months, mid March-mid July; summer teams: 7 weeks, mid July-September. Spring team members have the option of staying on to join a summer team project.

Participants are responsible for all travel and living expenses during the project. A rough guide to costs would be £1,470 for spring projects, £1,170 for summer projects, to cover travel, food, accommodation, insurance and pocket money. Advice given on raising funds. Accommodation is self-catering, and the same as that available to local people.

Compulsory orientation course held before departure, and reunion conference held in autumn/early winter

Full details of projects available 3 months before teams are scheduled to depart

LEONARD CHESHIRE FOUNDATION

Secretary to Personnel Adviser, The Leonard Cheshire Foundation, Leonard Cheshire House, 26-29 Maunsel Street, London SW1P 2QN

071-828 1822

Throughout the UK, though there are no Homes in Central London

A charitable trust founded in 1948, which now has some 260 Homes in 50 countries including over 80 in the UK. It has no boundaries of sex, creed or race, concerned only with the care of people with disabilities. The common aim of all Cheshire Homes is to provide care and shelter in an atmosphere as close as possible to that of a family home; residents are encouraged to lead the most active life their disabilities permit and to participate in the running of the Home and decisions affecting it.

Volunteers are needed in many Homes to assist with the general care of residents who require help in personal matters, including washing, dressing, toiletting and feeding, as well as with hobbies, letter writing, driving, going on outings or holidays and other recreational activities. Recruits some 100 volunteers annually.

Ages 18-30. Applicants must have an interest in and a desire to help the handicapped; the work is hard and requires understanding and dedication. Previous experience useful but not essential. Preference generally given to those planning to take up medical or social work as a career. Volunteers must be adaptable, dedicated, hard working, punctual and willing to undertake a wide variety of tasks.

3-12 months

Volunteers work a 39 hour, 5 day week. Board, lodging and at least £25 per week pocket money provided. Travel costs paid by volunteer.

Recruitment all year. More jobs available in summer than winter.

Annual Report; information leaflets

LOCH ARTHUR VILLAGE COMMUNITY

Admissions Officer, Loch Arthur Village Community, Camphill Village Trust, Beeswing, Dumfries DG2 8JQ

Kirkgunzeon (038 776) 687

Dumfriesshire, Scotland

A Camphill village community providing a home, work, further education and general care for approx 30 handicapped adults. The community consists of 6 houses, a farm, a vegetable garden, craft workshops and a 500-acre estate.

Volunteers are needed to live and work alongside residents in every aspect of life, including bathing, dressing and other personal tasks. Main areas of work are on the farm and in the garden, houses and workshops. Volunteers are also encouraged to take part in the community's cultural, recreational and social activities.

Ages 18+. Volunteers should be open, caring, enthusiastic and willing to help wherever they are needed. No previous experience or qualifications necessary.

12 month commitment preferred. Some short-term placements available in summer, minimum stay 6 weeks.

Full board accommodation provided in the community, plus pocket money

On-going instruction is given by experienced co-workers, plus formal introductory course sessions on a regular basis

Recruitment all year; apply at least 2 months in advance

L O T H L O R I E N   (R O K P A   T R U S T)

Project Manager, Lothlorien (Rokpa Trust), Corsock, Castle Douglas, Kirkudbrightshire DG7 3DR

Castle Douglas (06444) 602

South west Scotland

Established in 1978, Lothlorien consists of a large log cabin set in 17 acres of grounds containing vegetable gardens, woodland, fields, workshops and outbuildings.
It functions as a supportive community with everyone encouraged to participate in its daily running. The guiding principals of the community are hospitality, care and respect for the person, and a belief that the potential of the individual can be encouraged through communal life, to which all have a contribution to make. There is accommodation for fourteen people, including four volunteers.

Volunteers live and work alongside people who may have had a crisis in their lives through mental illness, stress, other mental, physical or emotional problems. Together with the permanent staff volunteers make up a core group who are responsible for day to day management and providing a continuity of support to residents.

Volunteers are sought with a caring, flexible and gregarious attitude. No previous experience or qualifications are necessary, but those with special skills are encouraged to use them where appropriate and to involve other residents in their activities.

Six months minimum

Board and lodging provided, and volunteers receive £25 per week pocket money

Training and supervision provided

Recruitment all year

MEDICAL AID FOR PALESTINIANS

Volunteer Officer, Medical Aid for Palestinians, 33A Islington Park Street, London N1 1QB

071-226 4114

Middle East: the Occupied Territories, Lebanon, Jordan and Egypt

A non-partisan, non-political registered charity established in 1984 in response to the massacres of Sabra and Shatilla, MAP is dedicated to improving the health conditions of Palestinian people by providing material, financial and personnel support to Palestinian health institutions.

Specialised medical personnel work on a variety of primary and secondary healthcare projects, including mother and child healthcare, physiotherapy and occupational therapy, community nursing, intensive care medicine and surgery, Approx 25 volunteers are recruited each year.

Applicants must have medical/nursing qualifications and practical hands-on medical experience. Some familiarity with development work is useful. They should be motivated by a concern for human welfare, culturally and politically aware, with a desire to learn and develop in a challenging environment. All nationalities considered; knowledge of English essential. B D PH W considered depending on project and practicalities.

Six months minimum.

Accommodation and a living allowance provided, plus full health insurance and return travel. There is also a monthly grant paid in the UK and a resettlement grant on completion of contract.

Compulsory briefing prior to departure. Prospective volunteers are also put into contact with previous volunteers wherever possible. On return, volunteers receive a project debriefing and are encouraged to share their experiences with others through talks and slide shows, as well as help with fundraising and appeals.

Apply 2-3 months in advance of a specific project commencing

Annual Review; Health in Gaza: A Casualty of Occupation; NGO Directory 1991; and *Laboratory Services in the Occupied West Bank and Gaza*

MERCY CORPS

The Director, Mercy Corps, Gwynedd Mercy College, Gwynedd Valley, Pennsylvania 19437, United States

(215) 641 5535

United States

Established in 1978, Mercy Corps is a volunteer lay ministry programme for women and men grounded in Christian values as witnessed by Catherine McAuley and the Sisters of Mercy. The three essential components of Mercy Corps are compassionate service, community and prayer. The primary focus of service is to the poor, sick and ignorant.

Corps members serve throughout the United States. There are positions for teachers, special education teachers, teachers' aides, nurses, physical and occupational therapists, houseparents, shelter staff, business and office administrators.

Ages 21+. Certain positions require professional qualifications and skills; some previous experience of voluntary service is preferred. Motivation to serve the people of God, flexibility and a sense of humour are essential characteristics. All nationalities welcome; applicants must be able to communicate fluently in English and arrange their own visas.

One year minimum, commencing August. Commitment may be renewed for a second year.

Accommodation, health insurance, work-related travel costs and return travel within the United States are provided by the site of service. Mercy Corps provides $100 per month stipend, $100 per month food allowance and $25 per month emergency fund.

Compulsory orientation held at Gwynedd Mercy College during the first week of August

Apply by 30 June

MISSION AVIATION FELLOWSHIP

The Manager, Candidates Department, Mission Aviation Fellowship, Ingles Manor, Castle Hill Avenue, Folkestone, Kent CT20 2TN

Folkestone (0303) 850950

Africa: Chad, Ethiopia, Kenya, Madagascar, Namibia, Tanzania, Uganda

A Christian organisation founded in 1947 and committed to helping the church in isolated areas by providing aircraft, pilots and the back-up that air transport work of this nature demands. The Fellowship aims to spread the Gospel, life and hope in spiritual and physical terms to thousands of people, providing an essential service to national pastors, church leaders, missionaries and medical and relief agency workers, by flying them to places where they are needed most. MAF also transport food, equipment, medical and agricultural supplies, emergency relief and other essential materials to remote and otherwise inaccessible locations, and are on call as an aerial ambulance service.

Pilots, aircraft engineers, avionics technicians and administrators are needed. Volunteers work in partnership with Christian and other organisations, forming a unifying link between individuals or families working at lonely outposts.

Ages 18+. Volunteers should have a Christian commitment and be active in the life of the church. Staff are selected for their skill, temperament and spiritual maturity. Pilots, aircraft engineers and avionics specialists must hold the appropriate licences and have relevant experience. Advice on the requirements and courses available will be given to those who would like to take up this opportunity for service to others.

Initially 3 years

Financial support on an agreed scales must be raised by sending churches and others interested in the applicants. The level of support covers salary, accommodation, car, travel to and from the UK and the place of work, medical care, and education for children where appropriate.

All personnel are given special training before they become active overseas to help them to adjust to cultural differences in the places where they will work. They also receive guidance on their return to the UK.

Applications can be made at any time

Annual Report; MAF News quarterly magazine

MISSIONS TO SEAMEN

The Ministry Secretary, The Missions to Seamen, St Michael Paternoster Royal, College Hill, London EC4R 2RL

071-248 5202

At some 20 seaports in Britain and around the world, including Brisbane, Dampier, Dunkerque, Fremantle, Hull, Immingham, Kobe, Liverpool, Marseille, Mombasa, New Orleans, Port Hedland, Rotterdam, Seaham, Singapore, Southampton and Yokohama.

An Anglican missionary society founded in 1856, caring for the spiritual, material and moral welfare of seafarers around the globe. The Missions help to combat isolation, exploitation and the dangers of the sea, working for improvements in conditions, education and welfare, serving seafarers of every race, colour and creed, offering a ministry of word, sacrament, counselling care and Christian welcome. The most important feature is the visit of the chaplain and staff to each ship on arrival in port.

There are volunteer service schemes for chaplain's assistants, providing an opportunity to be involved in practical Christian service within the shipping industry. Work is varied and involves visiting ships, conducting sightseeing tours, arranging sporting events, visiting hospitals, and helping with worship. Serving in the seafarers' centres can include bar and shop work, arranging video shows, telephone calls, gardening and cleaning. Recruits approx 26 volunteers annually.

Ages 18-24. Applicants should be sympathetic and understanding, good at quickly establishing relationships, prepared to befriend people of all nationalities and must have an interest in this particular form of ministry. No specific experience necessary, but the possession of a clean driving licence is required. Applicants must be members of a Christian denomination and prepared to participate full in Anglican ministry and worship. They need three suitable references.

One year, starting September

Board and lodging, travel costs, medical/accident insurance, approx £25 pocket money per week and 3 weeks holiday per year provided

One day debriefing on return

Completed applications should be sent before the end of March

Information leaflets; *Flying Angel News* newsletter; *The Sea* and *Prayer Union*

OCKENDEN VENTURE

The Personnel Officer, Ockenden Venture, Guildford Road, Woking, Surrey GU22 7UU

Woking (0483) 772012 Fax (0483) 750774

Barmouth, North Wales; Dewsbury, Yorkshire; Haslemere and Camberley, Surrey

Despite enormous international resettlement programmes there are still an increasing number of refugees throughout the world who are unable to find asylum. The Ockenden Venture is a charity founded in 1955, providing home, health, education and rehabilitation at home and abroad for refugees, displaced persons and casualties of conflict and oppression. The Venture also provides long-term care for a group of young handicapped refugees.

Volunteers are needed in the Venture's UK centres to work as general assistants with refugee families and as care assistants with mentally and/or physically handicapped young people, many of whom are refugees. Help is required with driving, cooking, property maintenance, creative activities and with the general care and welfare of the refugees.

Ages 18+. Applicants should be physically fit with a genuine desire to help and willingness to work hard. The houses are run on non-institutional lines in order to create homes, so volunteers are expected to accept a fair share of domestic work and responsibility. They must be able to work as a team member. Qualifications or experience not generally necessary. Current driving licence useful. All nationalities welcome. Fluent English essential.

Preferably 1 year, although occasionally there are shorter term engagements

Volunteers receive full board and lodging and a minimum of £22 pocket money per week. 23 working days' holiday per year, pro rata for shorter periods.

Recruitment all year, most volunteers join in August/September

OPTIONS

The Director, Options, Project Concern International, 3550 Afton Road, San Diego, California 92123

(619) 279 9690   Fax (619) 694 0294

Over 60 countries worldwide including Ghana, Kenya, India, Nepal, Pakistan, Thailand, Guatemala, St Lucia and Romania, as well as in 30 US states

Options is the international health recruitment and referral service of Project Concern International, a non-profit organisation working in primary health care training and development. Options provides professional volunteer opportunities linking health and development specialists with programmes, hospitals and clinics worldwide.

Hundreds of volunteers are placed each year, including primary care physicians, surgeons, nurses, physician assistants, dentists, lab technicians, health trainers, public health and hospital administrators, sanitation and water engineers.

Relevant health related qualifications and skills are essential, and previous overseas experience is preferred. Students should not apply. For positions in the United States, US credentials are required. Knowledge of languages depends on host country.

Short and long-term assignments, ranging from 1 month to 2 years

Options matches the applicant's job preferences to available positions. Terms and conditions are arranged between the volunteer and the facility, but will typically include housing and meals. Membership fee $25.

Follow-up evaluations conducted with each volunteer on completion of assignment

Recruitment all year

Bi-monthly newsletter lists current opportunities

PARADISE COMMUNITY

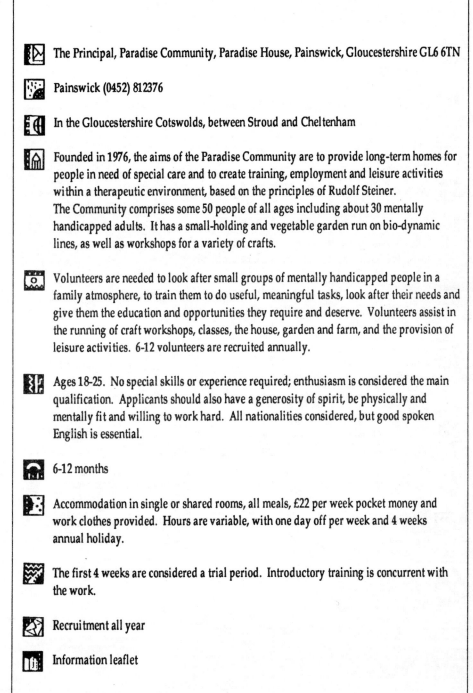

The Principal, Paradise Community, Paradise House, Painswick, Gloucestershire GL6 6TN

Painswick (0452) 812376

In the Gloucestershire Cotswolds, between Stroud and Cheltenham

Founded in 1976, the aims of the Paradise Community are to provide long-term homes for people in need of special care and to create training, employment and leisure activities within a therapeutic environment, based on the principles of Rudolf Steiner.
The Community comprises some 50 people of all ages including about 30 mentally handicapped adults. It has a small-holding and vegetable garden run on bio-dynamic lines, as well as workshops for a variety of crafts.

Volunteers are needed to look after small groups of mentally handicapped people in a family atmosphere, to train them to do useful, meaningful tasks, look after their needs and give them the education and opportunities they require and deserve. Volunteers assist in the running of craft workshops, classes, the house, garden and farm, and the provision of leisure activities. 6-12 volunteers are recruited annually.

Ages 18-25. No special skills or experience required; enthusiasm is considered the main qualification. Applicants should also have a generosity of spirit, be physically and mentally fit and willing to work hard. All nationalities considered, but good spoken English is essential.

6-12 months

Accommodation in single or shared rooms, all meals, £22 per week pocket money and work clothes provided. Hours are variable, with one day off per week and 4 weeks annual holiday.

The first 4 weeks are considered a trial period. Introductory training is concurrent with the work.

Recruitment all year

Information leaflet

PIÑA PALMERA

Anna Johansson, Centro de Atención Piña Palmera, Apdo Postal 109, Pochutla 70900, Oaxaca, Mexico

In the UK volunteers may apply through Jean Sinclair, 142 Cartington Terrace, Heaton, Newcastle-upon-Tyne, NE6 5SJ

Newcastle-upon-Tyne 091-265 4639 *(from March 1993)*

Mexico

A centre based in Zipolite village, in the Pacific coast state of Oaxaca, Mexico. Provides rehabilitation and medical services for local people, particularly disabled children and their families, including outreach work to surrounding villages.

Work includes caring for disabled children, organising children's activities, nursing, physiotherapy, speech therapy, building repair and maintenance, agriculture, carpentry, toy and hammock making. About 12 volunteers work at the Centre in any one year.

Ages 18+. Good level of spoken Spanish essential. Both qualified and unqualified volunteers are welcome. Previous relevant experience is useful but not essential. More important are adaptability, enthusiasm and a willingness to learn. B D PH W

Three months minimum for qualified volunteers such as nurses, speech therapists and physiotherapists. 6 months minimum preferred for other volunteers.

Accommodation provided if space available, otherwise volunteers find their own nearby or use tents (unsuitable during June-September rainy season). Communal meals provided. Volunteers must organise and finance their own travel, insurance and personal expenses.

Apply 2-3 months in advance

Quarterly newsletter

QUAKER PEACE AND SERVICE

Service Projects Secretary, Personnel Department, Religious Society of Friends, Friends House, Euston Road, London NW1 2BJ

Various countries

The Religious Society of Friends, which has 18,000 members in Britain is concerned for international understanding and world development, the promotion of human rights and the more equitable sharing of the world's resources.

Quaker Peace and Service recruits men and women to work overseas in teaching, community development, health, international affairs work and other areas as needs arise. There are only a limited number of opportunities.

Most recruits are qualified professionals with relevant skills, perhaps those thinking of early retirement. For one-year posts 20-26 year-olds with less work experience are considered. Applicants need not be Quakers, but must be in sympathy with the Society's beliefs and aims.

One, two or three years

Overseas workers receive a maintenance allowance and pocket money

Those selected for placement are prepared for service at Friends House, London, and Woodbrooke, the Quaker college in Birmingham

Apply at any time

REACH

 The Director, REACH, 89 Southwark Street, London SE1 0HD

071-928 0452

Throughout Great Britain

A registered charity founded in 1979 by a small group of executives from the business and voluntary sectors, who reasoned that retirement should be looked upon as the beginning of a new way of life and the chance of continuing to be active in the community, and were concerned that the potential resources of retired professionals were not being deployed to advantage. REACH arranges part-time, expenses-only jobs for retired (or redundant) people with business or professional expertise who want to work as volunteers in charities. Although it is willing to help to define problems and develop proposals in assessing the resources that are required, REACH does not initiate projects on its own.

Retired professional people are matched to charitable organisations where there is a need for the volunteer's skills which cannot be met in any other way, and where the task makes use of the business or professional skills requested. Skills in high demand include finance, management, marketing and public relations. In addition to placement in conventional voluntary organisations, there are also opportunities in the fields of arts, culture, environment, religion and sport. This job-finding service is offered free of charge to both volunteers and voluntary organisations. Some 700 volunteers placed each year.

No age restrictions, providing applicants can offer professional expertise gained during their working lives. They should have a desire to utilise their skills and experience for the benefit of the community, and adapt them according to the needs of the chosen charity. B D PH W

No limit on length of placement; volunteers work on average 2-3 days per week but this can vary from 1 day up to 5 days per week.

Applicants are asked to complete a Registration Form which includes details of their skills, the duration and amount of time they are willing to give, and geographical constraints. Work is usually part-time, and out-of-pocket expenses are paid.

After placement a 6-monthly follow up is carried out by letter

Recruitment all year; apply 2 months in advance

Annual Report; information leaflets; *To Shine in Use* video; *Reach Forward* newsletter

R I C H M O N D   F E L L O W S H I P

Personnel Department, Richmond Fellowship, 8 Addison Road, London W14 8DL

071-603 6373

Throughout the UK

A registered charity and Housing Association which has worked in the field of mental health since 1959. Now runs more than 50 community based projects in the UK working with people of all ages, and has its headquarters in London. The projects include intensive rehabilitation programmes, supported housing projects, group homes and workshops for people with mental health problems, schizophrenia, addiction and emotional problems. Work in the projects focuses on helping residents to regain personal stability, the ability to make good relationships and to find and keep a job. The Richmond Fellowship also runs its own colleges and provides a comprehensive range of training options for its own staff and for people involved in mental health and human relations work.

Volunteers are needed to work within some of the projects, side by side with the project staff, assisting the residents and helping in the day-to-day running of the house. As well as assisting with the basic necessities of life, some volunteers also become involved in activities such as gardening, cooking, art, music, drama and sport.

Ages 18+. Applicants should have the commitment to do what can be a very demanding but ultimately rewarding job, and the ability to relate sensitively and sensibly to the residents. Prior experience not essential, although previous knowledge of the mental health field is useful. More important is the genuine commitment and enthusiasm to become involved in a caring role. Skills in recreational activities an advantage.

Duration dependent on volunteer, although a reasonable time period is needed to become an effective part of the team

Volunteers usually become involved in a project in the locality in which they already live, therefore board and lodging are not generally provided. Hours are dependent on the volunteer's other commitments. Volunteers are expected to accept the obligations and codes of practice that apply to other staff members.

Recruitment all year. A list of projects is available; applicants should apply directly to the project(s) where they wish to work.

RICHMOND FELLOWSHIP INTERNATIONAL

International Secretary, Richmond Fellowship International, The Coach House, 8 Addison Road, London W14 8DL

071-603 2442   Fax 071-602 0199

Mainly US; opportunities may arise in Eastern Europe and developing countries

Founded in 1981, the largest international voluntary organisation working in the field of community mental health. Based on experience gained in the UK and elsewhere, the Fellowship provides a form of social therapy - the therapeutic community - in which clients are helped to re-enter society through a carefully designed programme of group activities and individual counselling. This form of social therapy is now an accepted part of psychiatric care. There are now 17 affiliates throughout the world providing psychiatric and drug rehabilitation services, and on-the-spot training.

Volunteers needed to work within projects, side by side with project staff, assisting with therapy and helping in day-to-day running. As well as assisting with the basic necessities of life, some volunteers also become involved in activities such as gardening, cooking, art, music, drama and sport. There may also be opportunities for administrative and financial workers. Senior volunteer positions may arise for consultants/trainers.

Ages 22+. Selection process identifies committed, capable and resilient volunteers. Applicants should be mature, have previous volunteer experience plus professional training in nursing, social work or psychology, particularly in the rehabilitation of psychiatrically and emotionally disturbed adults. They should also have practical skills in cooking, home making, art and recreational activities. Applications viewed creatively, and candidates are matched with the placement best suited to utilising their skills.

Twelve months

Volunteers are expected to accept the obligations and responsibilities which apply to staff members, including professional relationship with residents and responsibility within the structure. 48 hour week in shifts. Board, lodging, 28 days annual leave, stipend in local currency equivalent to £27 per week, full insurance and return airfare provided.

Applicants interviewed in the UK at their own expense; sometimes possible to arrange local interviews. Orientation may include prior placements on a UK project and a Richmond Fellowship College course.

Recruitment all year

Annual Report

SCOTTISH CHURCHES WORLD EXCHANGE

 The Volunteer Programme Coordinator, Scottish Churches World Exchange, 6A Randolph Place, Edinburgh EH3 7TE

031-225 8115

Africa, Asia, Central America, Europe and the Middle East

An agency of the Scottish Churches, managed by a Committee of representatives or observers from most of the major Christian denominations and a number of missionary societies

Placements are arranged with an overseas partner of one of the Scottish churches or agencies. Volunteers are placed according to their interests, skills and personality, and work on a project of their choice. Emphasis is placed on volunteers becoming part of the local church and community.

Ages 18+. Open only to candidates from Scottish churches or others in Scotland willing to work in a church-related post. Relevant skills and experience are welcome but not essential.

6-18 months, beginning August/September

Food, accommodation and pocket money are provided by the host and World Exchange. Volunteers are expected to try and raise at least £1,500 towards the cost of their placement, which represents about one third of the real cost.

Compulsory preparation courses consist of four days at Easter and a week in early summer. On return, volunteers have a medical check, debriefing, and are encouraged to attend a weekend conference for returned volunteers.

Preliminary interviews held October-December; final selection days January and February

S I M - U K

 Personnel Secretary, SIM-UK, Ullswater Crescent, Coulsdon, Surrey CR5 2HR

 081-660 7778

 Africa: Benin, Burkina Faso, Côte d'Ivoire, Ethiopia, Ghana, Kenya, Liberia, Niger, Nigeria, Senegal, Sudan
Asia: Bangladesh, Pakistan, Philippines
Latin America: Bolivia, Chile, Peru

 International organisation founded in 1893 as the Sudan International Mission, composed of evangelicals drawn from different denominations. Serves the Church of Jesus Christ in facilitating the fulfilment of His command to preach the Gospel and glorify God through church planting. In conjunction with mission-related church/other organisations, its ministries include evangelical outreach, theological education, famine and disaster relief, rural and community development, health care, and youth and literacy programmes.

 Personnel are generally required in development work for agriculturalists, engineers, water specialists and construction engineers; trades such as electricians and plumbers; medical and medical auxiliary duties; broadcasting and office work; youth work in urban areas; and teaching at schools for missionaries' children.

 Ages generally 25+. Most countries require specific skills and experience. Bible training necessary; Christian education and youth work experience desirable. Applicants must have a commitment to the Lord Jesus Christ and ministry skills, able to work on their own initiative and have the strength to surmount loneliness, cultural differences, financial limitations and other frustrations. Working as team members, they should have the ability to live, work and worship in close proximity to their co-missionaries; they usually learn the language of the people amongst whom they work and, as necessary, the official host language. Stamina and good health essential. All nationalities considered.

 Open-ended commitment. Short-term service 12-30 months; special service up to 1 year. Summer missionaries usually 2-3 months stay, but may be extended by mutual agreement.

 All funds including travel to the host country must be raised by the participant. Advice given on obtaining sponsorship.

 Compulsory orientation course, approx one week, held once a year in London, when the volunteer's readiness for service is evaluated in depth. Debriefing interviews on return.

 Apply before the end of the preceding calendar year, preferably in October

 SIM Now quarterly magazine

SIMON COMMUNITY

The Community Leaders, The Simon Community, PO Box 1187, London NW5 4HW

071-485 6639

London and Kent

Founded in 1963, committed to caring and campaigning for and with the homeless and rootless. Catholic founded and inspired, but ecumenical in action with members of all faiths and none. Residents are men and women, young and old, rejected by society and being without support have slipped through the net of the welfare state. A night shelter, community houses and a farmhouse comprise a tier system enabling residents to find the appropriate level of support at a particular point in time. A long-term caring, supportive environment is provided where the individual can regain self respect; for those who are temporarily homeless, there is provision for emergency stopover.

Volunteers live and work with the Community resident. Activities include helping residents obtain medical care and social security, referral to other organisations, cooking, fundraising and campaigning, housework, administration, group meetings, night duty, going to rough sleeping sites with tea and sandwiches to make contact with homeless people and helping at a night shelter. Non-residential openings for regular part-time volunteer co-workers for specific functions such as driving or street work. Emotionally demanding work, dealing with problems including alcoholism, drug addiction and psychiatric disorders; of particular interest to those seriously considering social work.

Ages 19+. Applicants should have a commitment to, and some perception of, the aims and philosophy of the Community. They should have a willingness to learn and adapt, the ability to relate and respond to people, and must be caring, sensible, mature and stable enough to take the burden of other people's problems while retaining their own balance. Volunteers should be capable of taking initiatives within the framework of a team, learning to cope with crises, so a sense of humour is an asset. Academic qualifications or experience not essential. All nationalities accepted. Good command of English necessary.

Three months minimum, 6 months or more preferred

Workers live alongside residents, sharing the same facilities, food and conditions; accommodation can be basic and rough. Pocket money £15 per week. Average 16 hour day; 1 day per week free. 10 days leave after 3 months, with leave allowance.

Volunteers are required to do a weekend's orientation before a decision is taken whether to accept or not. Training is given within the project.

Recruitment all year; apply 1 month in advance

Information leaflets; *Caring on Skid Row; No Fixed Abode; The Untouchables*

SIMON COMMUNITY (IRELAND)

The Recruitment Coordinator, Simon Community (National Office), PO Box 1022, Lower Sheriff Street, Dublin 1, Republic of Ireland

Dublin (01) 711606/711319

Cork, Dublin, Dundalk and Galway

A voluntary body offering support and accommodation to the long-term homeless at night shelters and residential long-stay houses in Cork, Dublin, Dundalk and Galway. Full-time work in Simon is demanding and involves a very full commitment to people who will be difficult and who will challenge the volunteer's motivation and feelings. It does not suit everyone, yet for those whom it does it can be a very rewarding and enriching experience.

Volunteers are required to work full-time on a residential basis, living-in and sharing food with residents, taking responsibility for household chores and working to create an atmosphere of trust, acceptance and friendship by talking and listening, and befriending residents.

Ages 18-35, older applicants considered. Applicants should be mature, responsible individuals with an understanding of, and empathy for homeless people. Tolerance and an ability to get on with people and work as part of a team are also essential. No experience or qualifications necessary. All nationalities welcome; good standard of spoken English essential.

3+ months; first month is probationary period

Volunteers work 3 days on and 2 days off, with 2 weeks holiday entitlement every 3 months. Full board and lodging on the project provided, plus a flat away from the project on days off. Volunteers receive an allowance of IR£32 per week; insurance provided, but not travel costs.

Training on-site is given by project leaders; formal training courses in aspects such as first aid may also be provided.

Recruitment all year

SKILLSHARE AFRICA

Recruitment/Selection Officer, Skillshare Africa, 3 Belvoir Street, Leicester LE1 6SL

Leicester (0533) 541862

Africa: Botswana, Lesotho, Mozambique and Swaziland

Established in 1990 after being part of International Voluntary Service, Skillshare Africa sends skilled and experienced people to work in support of development in southern Africa

Workers are recruited following requests from community groups, non-governmental organisations and government departments in the countries concerned. They contribute to every aspect of development including education, planning, construction, agriculture and health. Some 40-50 workers are recruited each year.

Ages 22-65. Applicants must have a recognised professional qualification and at least two years' work experience in an appropriate field. They must be committed to sharing their skills with others. All nationalities considered, provided they have right of re-entry into the EC or Czechoslovakia. B D PH W considered depending on conditions of work at the project.

Two years minimum

Workers are provided with housing and a salary in accordance with local levels. Insurance, National Insurance contributions and travel costs also covered.

Orientation course provided. Opportunity to discuss posting and related matters with UK staff on return.

Apply 3-6 months in advance

SOUTH AMERICAN MISSIONARY SOCIETY

Personnel Secretary, South American Missionary Society, Allen Gardiner House, Pembury Road, Tunbridge Wells, Kent TN2 3QU

Tunbridge Wells (0892) 38647

Spain, Portugal and Latin America: Argentina, Bolivia, Chile, Paraguay, Peru

Founded in 1844, the Society exists to encourage and enable the spreading of the Gospel of the Lord Jesus Christ in Latin America and the Iberian Peninsula through partnership with Anglican and other churches, and to initiate and respond to opportunities by mutual sharing of prayer, personnel and resources, with the purpose of being a servant, partner and communication bridge in response to Christ's commission to live out the Gospel among all people.

A variety of placements are available, including working with street children and orphanages in Brazil; practical involvement with local churches in Argentina; teaching at a Church school in Paraguay or Chile; and working with local Christian groups on evangelical outreach programmes in Spain. There are also opportunities for medical students to visit South America as part of their medical elective placement period. Approx 12 volunteers are recruited each year.

Ages 18+. Applicants must be committed Christians with the support and backing of their home church in Britain. They must also have a desire to extend their own personal experience in serving the national Church. Knowledge of Spanish or Portuguese very useful.

6-12 months

Volunteers are expected to contribute towards the cost of accommodation, which will be with other missionaries or with a host family. They must also raise their own return airfare, medical and travel insurance and living expenses, but some help may be given towards obtaining sponsorship.

Orientation not compulsory, but is sometimes arranged for long-term missionaries. Debriefing meeting and continued follow-up provided on return.

Recruitment all year; apply 4-6 months in advance

Information leaflets; *Share* quarterly newsletter

SUE   RYDER   FOUNDATION

The Administration Officer, Sue Ryder Foundation, Sue Ryder Home, Cavendish, Sudbury, Suffolk CO10 8AY

Glemsford (0787) 280252

England and Scotland

A charity founded in 1952 with over 80 homes throughout the world, primarily for the disabled and incurable, but also admitting those who, on discharge from hospital, still need care and attention. The aim is to provide residents with a family sense of being at home, each with something to contribute to the common good. Seeks to render personal service to those in need and to give affection to those who are unloved, regardless of age, race or creed. The homes are a living memorial to the millions who gave their lives during two world wars in defence of human values, and to the countless others who are suffering and dying today as a result of persecution.

Volunteers are needed at headquarters and sometimes in other homes. Work includes helping with patients, routine office work, assisting in the kitchen, garden, museum, coffee and gift shop at headquarters, general maintenance and other essential work arising. Experienced volunteers also needed for secretarial work and nursing.

Ages 16+. Applicants should be flexible and adaptable. A keen interest in caring work is desirable. Qualifications or experience not essential, but an advantage; preference given to students or graduates. Doctor's certificate required. All nationalities considered. Good standard of English required.

Two months minimum

Board, lodging and £10 per week pocket money provided

Two week trial period. On the job instruction provided.

Recruitment all year; larger number of volunteers required in summer

T E R R E N C E   H I G G I N S   T R U S T

Volunteer Coordinator, The Terrence Higgins Trust, 52-54 Grays Inn Road, London WC1X 8JU

071-831 0330

Greater London

A registered charity set up in 1983 to inform, advise and help on AIDS and HIV infection. The Trust currently involves over 1300 people, the vast majority of whom are volunteers. They provide help, advice, information, support and training not only to people with AIDS and HIV infection, but to anyone concerned about this health crisis.

Volunteers are required to work as Buddies, people who make a commitment to befriend someone with AIDS, contacting them at regular periods to talk, listen and help with practical tasks. Buddies may also act as mediators or advocates, helping the person with AIDS to access resources in the community. They are not nurses or carers, but friends. The Trust also needs volunteers to help provide a variety of other services, including counselling; a helpline; welfare, housing and legal advice; international liaison; drugs and prisons services; health education and information.

Ages 18+. All volunteers must have a commitment to the aims and activities of the Trust. Buddies do not need any previous experience or qualifications, but they must have a non-judgmental, non-discriminatory attitude and a respect for confidentiality. For other volunteer opportunities experience and qualifications may be required. As the work is not residential, volunteers must be based in the Greater London area.

One year minimum commitment

The Trust provides travel and lunch expenses where necessary as well as personal accident insurance

After an interview and Induction Training Day those considered suitable to be Buddies take part in an Intensive Residential Training Weekend which covers the issues which affect a Buddy's work. Buddies are also asked to attend follow up training sessions as well as monthly support and supervision groups.

Apply at any time

TIME FOR GOD SCHEME

 The Director, The Time For God Scheme, 2 Chester House, Pages Lane, London N10 1PR

 081-883 1504

 Throughout the UK

 A charity founded in 1965 and sponsored by the Baptist Union, United Reformed Church, Methodist Association of Youth Clubs, Congregational Federation, Baptist Missionary Society, National Council of YMCAs and the Church Army, and supported by the Church of England. Aims to offer young people the chance to explore their Christian discipleship through voluntary service in a supportive framework.

 Volunteers work in community centres, residential care homes, churches, hostels for the homeless, YMCAs and outdoor pursuits centres. Work can involve arranging activities for youth groups or residents; being good listeners at a community drop-in or at a lunch club for elderly people; visiting people and building up relationships; helping care for physically and mentally disabled children; and helping with typing and other administration. Some work in cities, others in rural and suburban areas. All projects are Christian-based. Recruits approx 60 volunteers each year. **B D PH W**

 Ages 17-25; overseas volunteers 18+. Volunteers are normally recommended by a local church, and need to be committed Christians or genuinely searching for a Christian faith, have a concern for others, be willing to accept the challenge of Christian service and wish to be involved in God's work in the world. Experience not necessary. Those with voluntary work experience can be placed in appropriately challenging placements.

 6-12 months

 Full board and lodging in private house, staff quarters or self-catering flat and £22 per week pocket money provided. Return fare home paid for initial visit, at the start, and every 3 months of service. 40 hour week, 1 week's leave after 3 months. UK volunteers pay nothing; home church invited to contribute £275 towards training costs (help given where this is not available). Overseas volunteers pay £475 to cover registration fee and training costs.

 3-4 day Preparation for Service Course; Mid-Service Course after 4 months; 2 day End of Service Gathering. The training programme is seen as an essential part of the voluntary service, it encourages reflection on the experience and the linking of faith and action. All volunteers receive support and supervision, and one or more visits during the year.

Starting dates are in September and January of each year. UK volunteers should apply 6 weeks-8 months in advance; overseas volunteers: 6-12 months in advance.

 Information leaflets; newsheet

UNITED NATIONS ASSOCIATION INTERNATIONAL SERVICE

The Recruitment Administrator, United Nations Association International Service, Suite 3a, Hunter House, 57 Goodramgate, York YO1 2LS

York (0904) 647799   Fax (0904) 652353

Africa: Burkina Faso, Mali
Latin America: Brazil, Bolivia
Middle East: West Bank and Gaza

UNAIS was established in 1953 to promote understanding between people of different nations, cultures, religions and languages, through a sharing of skills and an exchange of experiences. It aims to help combat poverty, fear and dependency by committing skilled human resources. It sends skilled personnel to work in certain Third World countries for community-based organisations which are working for change.

Recruits from a wide range of disciplines, such as nurses, midwives, agriculturalists, human rights researchers, documentalists, agro foresters, water specialists such as hydrogeologists and irrigation advisors, livestock technicians, community development workers and primary health care advisers.

Relevant qualifications, working experience and skills essential. Third World and community work experience an advantage. Knowledge of the relevant foreign language or the ability to learn a language essential. Applicants must have an understanding of development issues, in order to strengthen local development groups and help increase understanding between peoples. They also need to be adaptable to new ways of working and living. UK residents preferred as selection takes place in the UK.

Two years minimum

Accommodation, living allowance in relation to local costs, travel and insurance provided. Class 2 Volunteer Development National Insurance contributions paid. 20 days leave per year.

Compulsory orientation course arranged. Language training provided where necessary.

Recruitment all year

Annual Review; information leaflets; *Viva* quarterly magazine

UNITED NATIONS VOLUNTEERS (UNV)

The Executive Coordinator, United Nations Volunteers, Palais des Nations, 1211 Geneva 10, Switzerland

Geneva (022) 788 2455   Fax (022) 788 2501

In the UK apply to: United Nations Volunteers, VSO, 317 Putney Bridge Road, London SW15 2PN

081-780 2266

In 1992 UN Volunteer specialists and fieldworkers were serving in 115 countries: 42 countries in Africa, 33 in the Asia-Pacific region and 22 in Latin America-Caribbean. Some two thirds of all UNVs are at work in 45 countries classified as Least Developed; 80% are themselves citizens of developing countries and 20% come from the industrialised world.

In 1970 the Secretary-General of the United Nations recommended the establishment of a volunteer scheme which would operate within the UN System. UNV's main activity is to programme, deliver and administer suitably qualified, experienced and motivated personnel for international technical cooperation and humanitarian work in developing countries. Over 2,000 volunteer specialists and grassroots fieldworkers of more than 100 nationalities are currently assigned, in projects executed by organisations of the UN System such as FAO, ILO, WFP, UNIDO, UNICEF, WHO, UNDP, UNHCR and UNESCO; or by developing country governments; or by UNV itself.

With particular emphasis on facilitating community-based initiatives, the programme provides middle- and upper-level skills in a wide range of sectors such as agriculture, health, education, humanitarian relief and rehabilitation, the environment, and small industry. UNV specialists are drawn from 115 different professions and skilled trades, ranging from accountancy to zoology.

Ages 21+; most volunteers are aged between 29 and 39. Retired people are very welcome to apply. Applicants must have a first degree and preferably a postgraduate award or equivalent technical qualifications. 2 years' minimum work experience also required, several years preferable. Lengthy work experience in certain areas may be substituted for academic qualifications. Ability to work in English and/or French, Spanish, Arabic, Portuguese or relevant local language essential. Candidates must possess the motivation to help others and share skills on a peer basis at working level.

continued overleaf

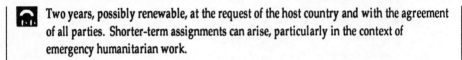 Two years, possibly renewable, at the request of the host country and with the agreement of all parties. Shorter-term assignments can arise, particularly in the context of emergency humanitarian work.

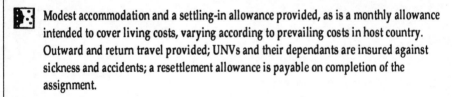 Modest accommodation and a settling-in allowance provided, as is a monthly allowance intended to cover living costs, varying according to prevailing costs in host country. Outward and return travel provided; UNVs and their dependants are insured against sickness and accidents; a resettlement allowance is payable on completion of the assignment.

Briefing may be provided in the UK, in Geneva, on arrival in the host country through the UN Development Programme Field Office, or by a combination of these.

Recruitment all year

UNV News quarterly; *UNV at a Glance* statistical information; *UNV Spectrum* providing update on roster of candidates every six months; also a general brochure

UNITED REFORMED CHURCH

The Personnel Secretary, World Church and Mission, The United Reformed Church, 86 Tavistock Place, London WC1H 9RD

071-916 2020   Fax 071-916 2021

Africa: Botswana, Madagascar, Zambia, Zimbabwe; Asia: Bangladesh, India; Caribbean: Jamaica; Far East: China, Hong Kong, Taiwan; Pacific: Kiribati, Papua New Guinea, Solomon Islands, Tuvalu, Western Samoa; Europe: Hungary, Italy, Romania.

Founded in 1972, a member of the Council for World Mission. Meets requests for staff from overseas partner Churches for their projects. Also involved in the international exchange of ministers, in arranging short-term volunteer appointments for young people with partner Churches in Europe, and in recruiting teachers of English for China.

Most requests are for lay missionaries working as secondary teachers, theological educators, doctors, nurses, accountants and occasionally administrators. They work alongside local people and are generally expected to run training programmes which allow national staff to assume greater responsibility. Opportunities in Europe for young people to work as volunteers in church institutions and to teach conversational English; in China, for qualified and experienced teachers of English for tertiary institutions.

Ages 18+ for short-term volunteer placements, 22+ for other placements. Unqualified volunteers are accepted for short-term opportunities in Europe; for other placements relevant qualifications, a few years of professional experience and a knowledge of relevant languages are required. Applicants should have a willingness to learn from overseas workers, sincerity in believing they can receive as well as share their skills, and a desire to share in the life and work of partner churches. B D PH W - applicants are treated on their merits, depending on requirements and facilities of placement.

3 months minimum for short-term placements; 2 years minimum for other placements.

For short-term opportunities volunteers meet their own travel costs and are provided with accommodation and minimum pocket money. For long-term placements accommodation and salary are in line with local workers and return travel is provided.

Compulsory preparation and orientation course for long-term appointments. Advice and help with reintegration given on return and, occasionally, specialist in-service and debriefing courses arranged. Short-term volunteers given preparation and advice.

Recruitment all year

Information leaflets

UNIVERSITIES' EDUCATIONAL FUND FOR PALESTINIAN REFUGEES (UNIPAL)

The Projects Officer, UNIPAL, 33A Islington Park Street, London N1 1QB

071-226 7997

Israeli-occupied West Bank and Gaza Strip; Palestinian communities in Israel, the Lebanon and Jordan

Founded in 1972, UNIPAL is a small educational charity which aims to provide forms of help which will benefit not only individuals but also Palestinian communities and especially over 700,000 refugees still in camps. Palestinian teachers of English are brought to the UK for training; financial aid is given to Palestinian educational institutions that are helping deprived children and young people; and volunteers are sent to the Middle East to share their skills.

A strictly limited number of volunteers are needed. Work involves providing English courses for Palestinian organisations, school children and teachers. There are also short-term summer opportunities helping in United Nations schools, children's homes and kindergartens.

Ages 22+ for long-term volunteers, 20+ for summer volunteers Applicants should have sensitivity, tolerance, readiness to learn, political awareness, adaptability and a sense of responsibility. TEFL Qualifications and previous relevant experience necessary for long-term volunteers. Background reading on the Middle East situation essential.

6-12 months; or 4-6 weeks for summer volunteers

Long-term volunteers receive accommodation, airfares, a living allowance and medical insurance; summer volunteers receive food and accommodation but pay their own fares, insurance and personal expenses

Interviews are held and successful applicants are then briefed on their placement

Recruitment all year. Selection and interviews for summer volunteers usually take place March-April.

UNIPAL News newsletter

UNITED SOCIETY FOR THE PROPAGATION OF THE GOSPEL

Short-Term Experience Programmes Officer, Mission Personnel Team, United Society for the Propagation of the Gospel, Partnership House, 157 Waterloo Road, London SE1 8XA

071-928 8681

Many countries worldwide, especially in the Third World

Founded in 1701, the Society enables the Church of England to relate effectively to Anglican and associate churches throughout the world and to support the work of overseas churches by offering them personnel, funding and bursaries.

Operates the Experience Exchange Programme, which was established to enable Christians from the UK to learn from the insights and experiences of Christians in other countries. Volunteer placements, agreed by local Anglican bishops and leaders of Christian community projects, assist in schools, medical centres, social welfare and agricultural projects. Recruits 30 volunteers annually. A small number of long-term personnel may also be required for work with the Church overseas; 3-year renewable contract.

Ages 18+. Applicants must be mature practising Christians with an interest and commitment in identifying with a local Christian community. They should also be adaptable to new situations, resourceful, sensitive to people and willing to suffer some hardship and loneliness. UK nationals only. No special qualifications or experience necessary. B D PH W

6-12 months, departing in July/August

Volunteers pay their own fares and insurance, and may be asked to contribute to board and lodging costs. Advice given on obtaining sponsorship.

Compulsory orientation courses arranged, with weekend debriefing and 24-hour personal debriefing on return home

Apply September-May

Annual Yearbook; information leaflets, videos and other resources. Catalogue available.

V I A T O R E S   C H R I S T I

The Secretary, Viatores Christi, 38 Upper Gardiner Street, Dublin 2, Ireland

Dublin (01) 728027/749346   Fax (01) 745731

Africa: Ethiopia, Gambia, Ghana, Kenya, Liberia, Malawi, Nigeria, Sierra Leone, South Africa, Tanzania, Zambia, Zimbabwe.   Asia: India, Pakistan.   Caribbean: Grenada, Haiti. Far East: Thailand.   Latin America: Argentina, Chile, Venezuela.   There are usually some volunteers involved in areas of need in Europe and North America.

A lay missionary association founded in 1960, dedicated to the active involvement of Catholic laity in the missionary work of the Church, with the task of recruiting, training and helping to place laity overseas in areas of need. It has the object of furthering the Church's work, of bringing Christ to people everywhere, and sharing skills in the process.

The most frequent requests are for teachers of all subjects; medical personnel including doctors, nurses and laboratory technicians; social workers; catechists; agriculturists; and mechanics, carpenters, builders, electricians and engineers. Some volunteers work as full-time pastoral, development or youth workers playing an active part in the local Christian community. Volunteers fulfil a specific task, in which they have training or experience, passing on their skills so that local people will be able to continue when they leave.

Ages 21+; training can be given before this age. Relevant skills and experience preferred. Volunteers should be concerned, caring and practising Catholics with a desire to share in Christ's mission and spread the Gospel. They should be open to learn, adaptable, have a sense of humour, be in good health and generally suited to the work to be done. Whether single or married, applicants should be free of family or other commitments. They should also be resident in Ireland, in order to attend training course.

One year minimum

Conditions depend on the requesting agency. Insurance, travel and usually board and lodging provided. Advice given on sponsorship.

Much emphasis is placed on the preparation programme, which comprises Christian formation, orientation and practical experience. Compulsory part-time orientation course lasts 9-12 months, depending on the individual's readiness and availability of a suitable post. As a debriefing service, residential weekends and seminars are held where experiences are shared: home involvement is invited.

Recruitment all year

International newsletter; *Annual Report*

VINCENTIAN SERVICE CORPS

The Director, Vincentian Service Corps, 7800 Natural Bridge Road, St Louis, Missouri 63121, United States

(314) 382 2800 ext 249

In England apply to: Vincentian Volunteer Coordinator, Christopher Grange, Youens Way, East Prescot Road, Liverpool L14 2EW

In Scotland apply to: Vincentian Volunteer Coordinator, St Vincent's Centre, 1 Middlepenny Road, Langbank, Renfrewshire PA 14 6XA

In Wales apply to: Vincentian Volunteer Coordinator, 106-7 Bryn Pinwydden, Pentwyn, Cardiff CF2 7DG

Midwestern United States: San Antonio, St Louis, Chicago, Indianapolis, rural Arkansas

A lay volunteer programme sponsored by the Daughters of Charity for men and women who want to serve the poor, live in community and experience a simple lifestyle.

Placements are generally in the fields of social services, education, health care and parish ministry, such as working as pastoral care staff in hospitals; nurses in clinics; teachers at schools; care providers for emotionally disturbed teenagers and people with physical handicaps; staff for transitional housing for the homeless; and parish staff working to meet the needs of inner city poor.

Ages 20+. Applicants must have a real desire to serve the poor, flexibility, a sense of identity, a sense of humour, an openness to living in community and a willingness to explore personal and spiritual growth through service. All nationalities accepted; fluent English required, and Spanish is useful in some areas.

One year minimum, beginning August

Accommodation provided, plus $100 per month stipend and $80 per month to cover food. Costs of health insurance and travel to and from St Louis to the placement site covered.

Compulsory 1 week orientation course held in St Louis in August

Apply before 15 June

VSC News newsletter for current and former volunteers

VOLUNTEER MISSIONARY MOVEMENT

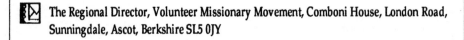

The Regional Director, Volunteer Missionary Movement, Comboni House, London Road, Sunningdale, Ascot, Berkshire SL5 0JY

Ascot (0344) 875380

The Regional Director, VMM Scotland, Gillis College, 113 Whitehouse Loan, Edinburgh EH9 1BB

031-452 8559

The Regional Director, VMM Ireland, High Park, Grace Park Road, Drumcondra, Dublin 9, Ireland

Dublin (01) 376565

Southern and eastern Africa: Bophutatswana, Kenya, Sierra Leone, South Africa, Tanzania, Uganda, Zambia, Zimbabwe

Founded in 1969 following the Second Vatican Council, VMM is an ecumenical movement within the Catholic Church which recruits, prepares and sends Christian volunteers with a skill or profession to work as lay missionaries in Catholic or other Christian mission projects linked with local churches. It is also involved in long-term development projects, mission awareness and development education in the UK.

Skilled volunteers are required to work in schools, hospitals, rural health centres, technical institutions and community development projects, where the aim is to help people help themselves. Work may be teaching, medical, administrative, pastoral, technical or agricultural. There are opportunities for experienced mechanics, builders, carpenters, plumbers, agriculturists, administrators, accountants, teachers of all subjects, nurses, midwives, doctors, laboratory technicians, pharmacists, physiotherapists and community development workers. Most volunteers work in rural areas which may be isolated, with limited social amenities. Recruits approx 40 volunteers annually.

Ages 21+. Applicants must have a Christian commitment, a concern for people and a desire to serve overseas motivated by a Christian faith. They need to be adaptable, stable and patient, capable of working independently, good at improvisation, with a sense of humour. Professional or technical qualifications required, plus at least 2 years' post-qualification experience in own trade or profession. Married couples without school-age children are accepted provided both are suitably qualified and available for work.

All nationalities considered; applicants must speak good English and be willing to learn the basics of the local African language.

Two years minimum

Basic board and lodging, small allowance in local currency and return air fare provided. Volunteers contribute £134 towards insurance.

Successful applicants attend weekend introductory course. Compulsory 5 week residential preparatory course arranged; volunteers contribute £75 towards cost. Open house for returned volunteers; weekends and retreats organised.

Recruitment all year. Application process can take several months before final acceptance; delays may also be experienced in obtaining work permits.

Newsletter; information leaflets; *VMM Spirit and Lifestyle* booklet setting out the Movement's role in the Church

V S O

 Enquiries Unit, VSO, 317 Putney Bridge Road, London SW15 2PN

 081-780 2266

 Africa: Egypt, The Gambia, Ghana, Guinea Bissau, Kenya, Malawi, Namibia, Nigeria, Sao Tomé & Principé, Sierra Leone, Tanzania, Uganda, Zambia, Zimbabwe
Asia: Bangladesh, Bhutan, Maldives, Nepal, Pakistan, Sri Lanka
Caribbean: Anguilla, Antigua, Dominica, Grenada, Montserrat, St Kitts, St Lucia, St Vincent, Turks & Caicos
Far East: Cambodia, People's Republic of China, Indonesia, Laos, Thailand
Latin America: Belize, Guyana
Pacific: Fiji, Kiribati, Papua New Guinea, Philippines, Solomon Islands, Tonga, Tuvalu, Vanuatu

 An independent organisation founded in 1958 with the aim of transferring practical experience, skills and expertise to developing countries. VSO enables men and women to work alongside people in poorer countries in order to share skills, built capabilities and promote international understanding and action in the pursuit of a more equitable world. Volunteers with relevant skills or qualifications are sent at the specific request of governments and local employers overseas, so that local counterparts can carry on the work once the volunteer's term of service expires. Volunteers are only sent to schemes which demonstrably help the appropriate community concerned, and all requests are evaluated against firmly established project criteria. There are more than 1,500 VSOs overseas at any one time working on projects in 50 developing countries.

 The majority of requests are in the following fields.
Primary, secondary and tertiary education: TEFL, teacher training, librarianship, special education, home economics, commerce and science.
Health: midwives, doctors, physiotherapists, health visitors, community nurses, pharmacists, dentists, laboratory technicians, occupational/speech therapists and nutritionists.
Technical trades, crafts and engineering: carpenters, bricklayers, joiners, plumbers, electricians, building instructors, mechanics, marine/civil engineers, technicians and technical teachers.
Agriculture: livestock and crop specialists, foresters, agricultural engineers, horticulturalists, animal health and production specialists, fisheries experts and agricultural science teachers.
Social, community and business development: advisors to help set up small business, establish craft workshops and cottage industries, community social workers and instructors working with disabled people, town planners and architects, communications

experts, systems analysts, journalists and solicitors.

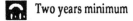 Ages 20-70; most volunteers are in their late 20s. Relevant qualifications essential, plus at least 2 years' relevant work experience. Applicants should have a genuine desire to assist in the long-term development of the developing world. They should be in good health, adaptable, prepared for life in a completely different culture, resilient in the face of frustrations, tolerant, have a sense of humour and a desire to combat all forms of exploitation. Couples without dependent children welcome, provided both partners have skills or qualifications acceptable to the programme and can be posted together. Volunteers should be living in the UK with unrestricted right of re-entry. **B D PH W**

Two years minimum

Accommodation provided by the host country. Volunteers live and work as members of the community, alongside their colleagues on similar pay. Air fare and other travel expenses, National Insurance contributions and payments to a specially arranged endowment plan plus medical insurance are provided. A further grant is paid on return.

Compulsory course arranged in which volunteers learn to adapt their skills to the needs of the host country, with briefing on the country, health care and any special training they may need by nationals and returned volunteers. Debriefing and advice on resettlement provided on return.

Recruitment all year; most volunteers are sent out in September and January. There is an average of 6-8 months between receipt of application and departure.

Orbit quarterly magazine; *Annual Review*; information literature

WORLDTEACH

Director of Recruiting, WorldTeach, Harvard Institute for International Development, One Eliot Street, Cambridge, Massachusetts 02138-5705, United States

(617) 495 5527   Fax (617) 495 1239

Africa: Namibia, South Africa
Asia: China, Thailand
Europe: Poland, Russia
Latin America: Costa Rica, Ecuador

WorldTeach was founded in 1986 with the goal of contributing to education overseas and creating opportunities for individuals to gain experience in international development. The administration of the programme is financed primarily by participants' fees, with additional contributions from the Harvard Institute for International Development, Harvard University, foundations and individual donors.

Most volunteers teach English as a Second Language, however, there are also opportunities to teach science, maths and sports. Establishments include primary and secondary schools, colleges and universities, non-profitmaking organisations and public enterprises, based in both urban and rural areas.

Ages 18+. Applicants must have a bachelors degree from an accredited college or university by their date of departure. Before leaving they must also have taken a course in Teaching English as a Second Language or have spent at least 25 hours teaching or tutoring English. Knowledge of the host country's language is helpful but not essential. Applicants should be independent and adaptable, with a commitment to teaching, and strong communication and interpersonal skills. All nationalities may apply, but fluency in English is required. B D PH W

One year minimum. Short-term programmes are available in China and South Africa.

Programme fee from $3,400 covers the cost of airfare from the US, health insurance, orientation and training and support during the year. Accommodation is provided with a host family or in a dormitory, and volunteers receive a small stipend equivalent to the pay of a local teacher. WorldTeach maintain a field representative in each country to assist in emergencies and help with any problems.

2-3 week orientation held on arrival in host country

Applications accepted at any time, the earlier the better

SECTION VI

PROFESSIONAL
RECRUITMENT

ACORD

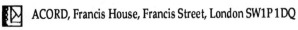

ACORD, Francis House, Francis Street, London SW1P 1DQ

071-828 7611

Various countries throughout Africa

A charity founded in 1976, a consortium of eighteen European and Canadian non-governmental organisations whose main role is to respond to development needs in areas of Africa where collective action is deemed more appropriate than separate action by individual member agencies and in circumstances where local agencies are not available for implementation of projects. The consortium is independent of political and religious affiliations, and plans and implements medium and long-term development programmes designed to promote the self-reliance of the communities concerned.

Specialists are needed in rural development including crop production, animal husbandry, small businesses and cooperatives

Personnel recruited must have several years' experience of working in the Third World

Reasonable professional salaries with benefits such as free housing, health insurance, annual leave and return travel provided

Information leaflet

BRITISH RED CROSS SOCIETY

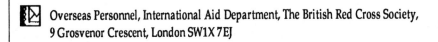

Overseas Personnel, International Aid Department, The British Red Cross Society, 9 Grosvenor Crescent, London SW1X 7EJ

071-235 5454

Mainly Africa and Asia

Founded in 1870, an independent voluntary organisation and part of a worldwide non-political, non-religious movement based on the fundamental principles of humanitarianism, neutrality and impartiality. As part of the International Red Cross, it has a statutory obligation to work for the improvement of health, the prevention of disease and the mitigation of suffering throughout the world.

Recruits salaried personnel, mostly qualified and experienced health workers, engineers, nutritionists, mechanics, logistics experts and experienced relief and development workers to work with the International Red Cross usually on emergency relief programmes for victims of natural disaster and conflict.

Applicants must be resident in the UK, with relevant qualifications and experience
B D PH W

Contracts are from 3-18 months

Salary, accommodation, travel, insurance and field allowance provided

Red Cross News quarterly newsletter; *The Red Cross Then and Now; Annual Review;* International Red Cross publications concerning relief and development work

HEALTH UNLIMITED

The Administrator, Health Unlimited, 3 Stamford Street, London SE1 9NT

Africa, Asia, Latin America

Health Unlimited works to develop sustainable primary health care systems with threatened communities which are isolated by conflict and its aftermath or suffer from discrimination.

Provides expert teams of medically qualified personnel to train trainers of community health workers and enable them to set up and run health systems at district and provincial level in developing countries. Some 10-15 people are recruited each year.

Only experienced, professionally qualified medical personnel or health educationalists are recruited. Applicants must have experience in developing countries, as well as a commitment, knowledge of development and sensitivity to the communities with whom they will be working. Knowledge of French of Spanish recommended.

Nine months-2 years, depending on project.

Personnel are paid at a rate of £600 per month for the first year, and £660 per month for the second year. Flights, insurance and accommodation provided.

Runs a 3-day Learning to Teach course 3 times a year in which recently enrolled team members may take part. Briefing provided to team members before they join a project, and debriefing on their return.

Apply in writing 6-12 months in advance

HELP THE AGED

Personnel Department, Help the Aged, St James' Walk, London EC1R 0BE

071-253 0253

Recruitment mainly for programmes in African countries, including Sudan, Tanzania and Mozambique; also in Asia: Cambodia

Founded in 1961, Help the Aged exists to meet the needs of frail, isolated and poor elderly people in the UK and overseas, responding to those needs with effective fundraising and aid programmes and by promoting a better awareness and understanding of them. Fundamental to the work is the belief that the world's aged should be able to live full lives as integrated members of society. Priorities in international programmes include self-help programmes for the urban poor, ophthalmic training, development of national age-care agencies and emergency and refugee relief. Primarily a funding rather than operational agency, financial support is given to self-help projects in over 60 countries.

Ophthalmologists and ophthalmic nurses are recruited to work alongside counterpart staff in programmes with a strong training element. Occasionally engineers/mechanics are needed to work on building projects or for maintenance of equipment and vehicles.

Applicants should preferably be over 25, with ophthalmic qualifications essential for relevant posts. Good UK experience necessary, preferably including some experience of training. Experience of work in developing countries also desirable, as is a willingness to learn the local language. Applicants should be adaptable, self-motivated, work well in a multi-cultural environment, committed to the principles of social justice and to helping the poor and vulnerable.

1-2 years, depending on the post

Reasonable salary is offered, normally tax-free. Accommodation is free, usually shared, and of a basic but reasonable standard.

A comprehensive briefing which normally lasts about 2 weeks is arranged before departure

Recruitment at different times of the year, depending on programme needs

Annual Report; Ageways; AgeAction; range of leaflets and other materials available

OVERSEAS DEVELOPMENT ADMINISTRATION

Overseas Development Administration, Room AH353, Abercrombie House, Eaglesham Road, East Kilbride, Glasgow G75 8EA

East Kilbride (0355) 844000

Caribbean, Latin America, the Pacific, Asia and Africa

Responsible for administering the British Government's programme of aid to developing countries. Also assists in the recruitment of specialists for the field programmes of the United Nations and its specialised agencies such as FAO and the International Labour Office, as well as for its Junior Professional Officer Scheme.

Vacancies occur on an *ad hoc* basis for graduates in natural science, education, engineering, accounting, law, medicine and veterinary science and are normally advertised in the national press and relevant professional journals

Substantial postgraduate experience is normally required, but postgraduate study awards are also offered. B D PH W all overseas appointments are subject to medical clearance.

Vacancies are usually for 2-3 year contracts

Recruitment all year. Enquiries stating brief personal details and requests for booklets should be sent to the above address, quoting reference number AH353/VW.

A number of useful free booklets such as *Opportunities Overseas in International Organisations, Why Not Serve Overseas, Careers in the Geological Sciences, Opportunities in Education Overseas* and a booklet outlining the *Associate Professional Officers Scheme* are available on request

O X F A M

Overseas Personnel Officer, Oxfam, 274 Banbury Road, Oxford OX2 7DZ

Oxford (0865) 311311

Africa, Asia, Latin America and the Caribbean, Middle East

Oxfam is a funding agency that exists primarily to provide finance for work to relieve and prevent suffering overseas, and to aid development. It does not itself normally carry out this work by sending expatriate personnel overseas, but prefers to operate by distributing money and resources through other organisations, agencies and local groups which have their own programmes in the field. It therefore only occasionally possible for Oxfam to offer employment for work overseas.

Maintains a retrieval register of qualified people able to work overseas, mainly for emergency relief postings in the areas of health, water or logistics; or advisory posts, for example in primary health care programmes.

Vacancies are for people with specialist skills and qualifications, and previous relevant overseas experience. There is no demand for unqualified and unskilled staff. Full driving licence essential; language ability useful. Personnel must be fit and healthy, and prepared to live under what may be very difficult conditions, often in extreme climates.

The register includes those looking for 1-4 year contracts, as well as those available to go overseas at short notice in response to an emergency, usually on 6 month contracts. Before joining the register applicants should ensure that they would be able to leave their present employment at short notice.

Oxfam meets all travel costs and pays a salary roughly compatible to the NHS at the lower levels for qualified staff. Depending on circumstances all accommodation and food costs are met or an allowance is allocated to cover them.

WORLD VISION OF BRITAIN

Personnel Manager, World Vision of Britain, Dychurch House, Abington Street, Northampton NN1 2AJ

Northampton (0604) 22964

Africa: Malawi, Mali, Mauritania, Mozambique, Senegal, Somalia, Zimbabwe
Asia: Cambodia, Vietnam
Europe: CIS/Russia, Romania

Founded in 1950, a branch of World Vision International, an inter-denominational Christian humanitarian organisation dedicated to serving God through childcare, emergency relief, community development, Christian leadership training and mission challenge. Operates in over 70 countries through local churches and community leaders in close cooperation with the United Nations and other international relief agencies.

World Vision seeks to employ local staff wherever possible and will only recruit staff to send overseas if it has not been possible to find a suitably-qualified person locally. They may recruit doctors, nurses, nutritionists, logisticians, hydrogeologists, civil engineers, water drilling experts and vocational instructors.

Applicants must have Christian commitment, relevant skills, qualifications and experience, knowledge of French or Portuguese and usually at least 3 years previous experience of working in the Third World. B D PH

One year minimum

Salary based on US scales, board, lodging, travel and insurance provided

Orientation course provided

Window on the World quarterly magazine; *Annual Report*; leaflets giving information on various issues

CHRISTIAN SERVICE CENTRE

Holloway Street West, Lower Gornal, Dudley, West Midlands DY3 2DZ

A member organisation of the Evangelical Missionary Alliance and the Evangelical Alliance, offering information and advice to those interesting in doing long-term Christian Service.

Matches the personnel needs of missions and Christian organisations in Britain and abroad with the availability of those offering themselves for service, and also provides a counselling and advisory service for prospective workers.

Advice is offered through a national network of advisers with experience of Christian work at home or overseas

Jobs Abroad directory of over 3,000 opportunities of interest to Christians, published twice a year; *STS Directory* yearly manual of short-term Christian service opportunities in the UK and abroad; *Who Needs You?* information on opportunities for voluntary Christian service for those working from home

CHRISTIANS ABROAD

 1 Stockwell Green, London SW9 9HP

 071-737 7811

 An ecumenical body founded in 1972 and supported by aid and mission agencies. Provides an information and advisory service on work abroad to help volunteers, of any faith or none.

It exists to encourage people to consider whether they have skills that would be welcomed abroad or something to contribute towards development and justice through study and action within the UK.

 Information and advice about openings through a variety of organisations, for those with or without professional and technical skills. Christians going abroad can be helped to find contacts with churches overseas and be put in contact with an adviser who has worked in the area. Assistance is offered to those returning from abroad who face the challenge of sharing their experiences and of using what they have learnt, and surmounting the problems of readjustment. A brief outline of qualifications, experience and interests should accompany any enquiry.

 A *Place for you Overseas* series of leaflets cover openings through many organisations and schemes. *Opportunities Abroad*, a six-monthly list of current vacancies through about 40 of the volunteer mission agencies with which Christians Abroad are in touch. *A Place for you in Britain* cover openings in the UK as a volunteer.

COORDINATING COMMITTEE FOR INTERNATIONAL VOLUNTARY SERVICE

 1 rue Miollis, 75015 Paris, France

 (1) 45 68 27 31/32

 A non-governmental international organisation founded in 1948 on the initiative of UNESCO, with a membership of over 100 organisations engaged in volunteer work, including those from eastern and western Europe, Latin America, Africa and Asia.

Through the promotion and development of the voluntary movement on regional, national and international levels the Committee works towards peace, international understanding, development and the furtherance of the efforts of developing countries in strengthening their national independence, and in solidarity with people in observance of the Universal Declaration of Human Rights. Works for the benefit of people affected by all forms of social and economic exploitation, unemployment, bad working and living conditions and promotes awareness and action against these forms of degradation.

Organises seminars and conferences, sponsors training courses for volunteer workers, participates in solidarity action and raises funds for concrete projects carried out by voluntary organisations in order to attain genuine development.

 CCIVS replies to requests for information received from individuals and organisations

 Directory of Organisations Concerned with International Voluntary Service; Volunteering in Literacy Work a guide to national and international opportunities; *News From CCIVS* regular bulletin

EVANGELICAL MISSIONARY ALLIANCE

Whitefield House, 186 Kennington Park Road, London SE11 4BT

071-735 0421

Founded in 1958, EMA is a fellowship of evangelical missionary societies, agencies, training colleges and individuals committed to world mission. Aims to encourage cooperation and provide coordination between member societies and colleges, and assist local churches to fulfil their role in world mission.

Provides a forum in which experiences, ideas and strategy can be shared; groups covering Africa, Asia, China, Europe, Latin America and the Muslim world meet regularly. Missionary exhibitions, conferences, visits and specialist training courses arranged.

As a clearing house for information on world mission it will assist enquirers and direct them to relevant sources. Also provides information on vacancies among member societies and colleges.

World Prayer News bi-monthly prayer bulletin; *EMA Newsletter* information digest; pamphlets and books on mission topics

RETURNED VOLUNTEER ACTION

 1 Amwell Street, London EC1R 1UL

 071-278 0804

 The only British organisation of and for prospective, serving and ex-volunteers and others who have worked overseas, existing independently from the sending agencies. It believes that a period of voluntary service abroad fails to achieve its full value unless it becomes part of an educative process for the volunteer, and much of its work involves face to face contacts between more recently returned volunteers and those who have been back for up to two years.

Provides information and advice for those thinking about volunteering overseas, a link with volunteers in Europe through Ex-Volunteers International, and helps returned volunteers to make use of their overseas experience in Britain by providing support and advice, training courses in communication skills and a channel through which volunteers can comment on and influence the policies of the sending agencies.

 Gives advice on all aspects of volunteering abroad and action to take on returning from a period of service. Provides information on alternative options for people unable to find development work placements overseas.

Working Overseas advisory pack containing information on the sending agencies and general advice for the prospective overseas worker, *Questioning Development, Handbook for Development Workers Overseas, Thinking About Volunteering?* and *The EVI Charter; Comeback* quarterly magazine; *Development Action* monthly bulletin; pamphlets and information sheets

SECTION VIII

UK & IRELAND
VOLUNTARY SERVICE:

A D V I S O R Y

B O D I E S

NATIONAL ASSOCIATION OF VOLUNTEER BUREAUX

 St Peter's College, College Road, Saltley, Birmingham B8 3TE

 021-327 0265

Volunteer bureaux aim to help people overcome the obstacles which might prevent them volunteering, whether this be a lack of information or a stereotyped view of what volunteering entails. Their central concern is the welfare of volunteers themselves and the development of volunteering in their local area. NAVB was set up in 1986 to increase public awareness of volunteer bureaux and to assist in their establishment and development.

Provides an information service on matters relating to volunteering. Enquirers can be put in touch with their local volunteer bureau, who will be able to advise them of the entire range of volunteer work available locally.

Volunteer Bureaux Directory

NATIONAL SOCIAL SERVICE BOARD

 71 Lower Leeson Street, Dublin 2

 Dublin (01) 616422   Fax (01) 746908

 Re-established by the National Social Service Board Act, 1984 to advise the Irish Minister for Health on the development of social services generally and to promote, encourage and resource services which disseminate information and advice to the public.

The Board also has statutory responsibility for the promotion of greater public awareness of, and accessibility to social services, and for the support of other bodies as specified by the Minister.

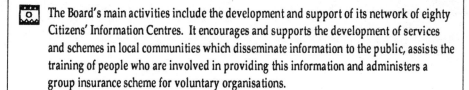 The Board's main activities include the development and support of its network of eighty Citizens' Information Centres. It encourages and supports the development of services and schemes in local communities which disseminate information to the public, assists the training of people who are involved in providing this information and administers a group insurance scheme for voluntary organisations.

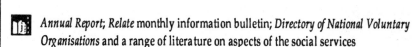 *Annual Report; Relate* monthly information bulletin; *Directory of National Voluntary Organisations* and a range of literature on aspects of the social services

NORTHERN IRELAND VOLUNTEER DEVELOPMENT AGENCY

Annsgate House, 70-74 Ann Street, Belfast BT1 4EH

Aims to promote volunteering throughout Northern Ireland and provides a central resource of support, information and training for all those involving volunteers, whether they are voluntary organisations, statutory agencies, communities or self-help groups.

The Agency provides a forum for all those involved with volunteering; practical support for projects involving volunteers; information and advice on issues relating to volunteering; training courses and materials for those who work with volunteers; and a focus for research and evaluation of current trends, policy and practice in volunteering.

Provides advice and information on where to apply in Northern Ireland for volunteer opportunities

Residential Volunteer Opportunities in Northern Ireland

SCOTTISH COUNCIL FOR VOLUNTARY ORGANISATIONS

 18-19 Claremont Crescent, Edinburgh EH7 4QD

 031-556 3882

 An independent national council with the prime objective of promoting and supporting voluntary service and action throughout Scotland, enabling other voluntary organisations to be effective. It extends the range of voluntary endeavour, advocates particular issues, promotes and safeguards the values of voluntary endeavour and provides services to these ends.

 Information and referral services

 Various, including two directories: *Community Organisations in Scotland* and *National Voluntary Organisations for Scotland; Inform* fortnightly current awareness bulletin; *Third Force News* fortnightly newsletter

VOLUNTEER CENTRE UK

29 Lower King's Road, Berkhamsted, Hertfordshire HP4 2AB

Berkhamsted (0442) 873311   Fax (0442) 870852

The Centre can provide information for those who want to volunteer for the first time, or for those who are already involved and want to know more. It runs events and training courses for those responsible for organising volunteers and coordinates UK Volunteers Week which takes place annually in June.

Extensive library and free information service. *Signposts* database on volunteering in the UK.

Volunteers journal published 10 times a year

WALES COUNCIL FOR VOLUNTARY ACTION

 Llys Ifor, Crescent Road, Caerphilly, Mid Glamorgan CF8 1XL

 Caerphilly (0222) 869224

 Formerly the Council of Social Service for Wales, WCVA is an independent national organisation established to promote, support and facilitate voluntary action and community development in Wales. It provides through the work of its staff and committees a service of information, advice and consultancy to all voluntary organisations which seek assistance, including funding advice; an intelligence service by monitoring developments in the voluntary sector in Wales and throughout the UK, as well as in government policies and current trends in society; an educational programme through the provision of a range of educational events from conferences to workshops; a representational role by responding to government consolations, taking the initiative to bring into the forum of public debate issues of importance for the development of voluntary action in Wales; a Volunteering in Wales Fund; and assists in the development of new projects which will link voluntary, statutory and commercial resources towards work creation and new forms of community benefit.

 The information service directly responds to enquiries from all those with an interest in voluntary organisations in Wales

 Network Wales monthly newsletter; *WIN Directory 1991* directory of national voluntary organisations in Wales; *A Short Guide to Voluntary Work Opportunities in Wales* information sheet; *Wales Funding Handbook*; Annual Report; general and funding information sheets; briefing papers

SECTION IX

SHORT-TERM
VOLUNTARY WORK

SHORT-TERM VOLUNTARY WORK

This guide's primary aim is to provide information and advice on medium (6-12 months) and long-term (1-2+ years) volunteer opportunities. However, you may be unable to commit yourself for such periods of time, not yet have the necessary skills/qualifications required on many longer-term placements, or if you have never undertaken voluntary work before, particularly outside your own country, you may wish to participate in a short-term project to gain experience. The options for short-term voluntary work are discussed in Section I, and further opportunities are detailed under Understanding Development.

Outline details of short-term voluntary projects, ranging in length from a weekend to six weeks, are given below. Comprehensive information on short-term voluntary placements in over 50 countries worldwide is given in the annual guide *Working Holidays,* see under *Information Resources.*

International workcamps are a form of short-term voluntary service providing an opportunity for people of different racial, cultural and religious backgrounds to live and work together on a common project providing a constructive service to the community. By bringing together a variety of skills, talents and experiences from different nations, volunteers not only provide a service to others but also receive an opportunity for personal growth and greater awareness of their responsibility to the society in which they live and work. Workcamp participants have an opportunity to learn about the history, culture and social conditions of the host country and to partake in the life of the local community.

Workcamps generally run for periods of 2-4 weeks, April-October; some organisations also arrange camps at Christmas, Easter and at other times throughout the year. Workcamp participants need to be mature enough not to require supervision and should be prepared to take responsibility for the successful running of the projects, group recreation activities and discussions. The minimum age is 17/18, with the exception of a number of youth projects, with a minimum age of 13.

The type of work undertaken varies considerably depending on both the area and the country in which the camp is being held. The work can include building, gardening and decorating, providing roads and water supplies to rural villages or constructing adventure playgrounds, and is within the capacity of normally fit volunteers. Virtually all workcamp organisers will consider volunteers with disabilities providing the nature of the work allows their active participation. Any manual work undertaken is usually for 7-8 hours a day, 5 or 6 days a week.

Workcamps can also involve community or conservation projects with work other than that of a manual nature. A few camps have shorter working hours and an organised study programme concerned with social problems or dealing with wider international issues.

Accommodation is provided in a variety of building such as schools, community centres or hostels, and may sometimes be under canvas. Living conditions and sanitation vary considerably and can be very basic; in some cases running water may not be readily available. Food is generally provided, although it is often self-catering, with volunteers preparing and cooking their own meals, sometimes on a rota basis. In many camps meals will be vegetarian.

Most workcamps consist of 10-30 volunteers from several countries. English is in common use as the working language, especially in Europe; the other principal working language is French. A knowledge of the host country's language is sometimes essential, especially for community work.

Workcamp applicants will generally pay a registration fee and arrange and pay for their own travel and possibly insurance.

Most workcamp organisers operate on an exchange basis with organisers in other countries. In some cases, especially with regard to workcamps in eastern Europe, the registration fee is higher in order to support the cost of the exchange. Volunteers may occasionally be expected to make a contribution towards the cost of their board and lodging, and should take pocket money to cover basic needs.

Although many organisations provide insurance cover for their volunteers, this is often solely against third party risks and accidents. Volunteers are strongly advised to obtain precise details on this and, where necessary, take out individual policies against illness, disablement and loss or damage to personal belongings. In addition to the compulsory vaccinations required for foreign travel, anyone joining a manual workcamp programme is strongly advised to have an anti-tetanus injection.

It is quite usual for workcamp organisations to hold day or weekend orientation seminars prior to volunteers going abroad. In some cases, especially for workcamps held in East European or Third World countries, attendance at these seminars is essential. Prospective volunteers will be able to learn a lot about aspects of voluntary work in the relevant countries as well as gaining background information on politics, culture and the way of life.

The following organisations run workcamps in the UK and also recruit volunteers for workcamps run by partner organisations overseas:

International Voluntary Service, Old Hall, East Bergholt, Colchester, Essex CO7 6TQ. The British branch of Service Civil

International, a network of workcamp organisers promoting international reconciliation through work projects.

Christian Movement for Peace, Bethnal Green United Reformed Church, Pott Street, London E2 20F *Ⓒ* 071-729 7985. An international movement open to all who share a common concern for lasting peace and justice in the world.

Concordia (Youth Service Volunteers) Ltd, 8 Brunswick Place, Hove, Sussex BN3 1ET *Ⓒ* Brighton (0273) 772086. Aims to bring together the youth of all nations to promote a better understanding between them of their ideas, beliefs and ways of living.

Quaker International Social Projects, Friends House, Euston Road, London NW1 2BJ *Ⓒ* 071-387 3601. Aims to promote cooperation and understanding through non-violent methods; to support community initiatives; to enable people from different cultures to live together; to facilitate personal growth, the acquisition of skills and a sense of personal responsibility. Applicants for workcamps abroad must be over 18 with previous workcamp or voluntary service experience.

United Nations Association International Youth Service, Temple of Peace, Cathays Park, Cardiff CF1 3AP *Ⓒ* Cardiff (0222) 223088. Aims to assist in community development by acting as a means to stimulate new ideas and projects, encouraging the concept of voluntary work as a force in the common search for peace, equality, democracy and social justice.

Workcamp Organisers lists nearly 280 national and international voluntary service organisations sponsoring workcamps in approx 90 countries. It includes the duration of the camps, months in which they take place, type of work, financial conditions and other details. Published every three years in cooperation with the Youth Division of UNESCO by the Coordinating Committee for International Voluntary Service, UNESCO, 1 rue Miollis, 75015 Paris, France. Cost FF12 or 14 IRCs. Also publish a *Camp Leader's Handbook*, cost FF12 or 14 IRCs.

International workcamps are generally concerned with community and social schemes, but short-term voluntary work may also be undertaken on archaeological, conservation or environmental projects.

Archaeology Sitting in the bottom of a trench for hours on end, carefully brushing away decades of deposits is not everyone's idea of pleasure, but involvement in a project that may discover important finds of Palaeolithic, Bronze Age or Roman habitation has particular rewards. The range of archaeological projects is immense; typical opportunities include studying the life of Magdalenian reindeer hunters through the excavation of Upper Palaeolithic sites in France; working on Roman, Anglo-Saxon and medieval city sites in Britain; excavations of a castle and village with Crusader, Mamluk and Ottoman remains in Israel; and uncovering the skeletons of bison killed by Native Americans over 9,000 years ago in Nebraska.

Although complete beginners are welcome on many excavation sites, applicants for archaeological work are often expected to have a formal interest in history or the classics, or to be studying archaeology at college or university level. It is also important to realise that on most excavations overseas, the site directors prefer to recruit those with experience; this is best first acquired on sites in your own country. Archaeological work can be hard and may continue in almost all weathers, and participants should be prepared accordingly. Any relevant skills should be made clear when applying; those with graphic, topographic or photographic skills are often particularly welcome. Beginners will usually receive board and lodging in return for their labours. Wages and/or travelling expenses may be offered to more experienced volunteers. Basic accommodation is normally provided, but volunteers may have to take their own tents and cooking equipment. The minimum age for participants is usually 18; those under 18 may be welcome provided they can produce a letter giving parental consent or if they are accompanied by a participating adult. Families may also participate on some projects. Work may be available almost all year round, but owing to the nature of the work, projects are most often undertaken in the summer season. Anyone involved in excavation work is strongly advised to have an anti-tetanus injection beforehand.

The Council for British Archaeology, 112 Kennington Park Road, London SE11 6RE © 071-582 0494 publishes the bi-monthly *British Archaeological News* which lists sites where volunteer helpers are needed, giving details of location, type and accommodation. Annual subscription £10.50 (UK) or £11.50 (Europe).

Archaeology Abroad, 31-34 Gordon Square, London WC1H 0PY provides information on opportunities for archaeological fieldwork and excavations outside Britain; full details are given in three annual bulletins.

Conservation work The Earth is 4,600 million years old; over the last 150 years we have come close to upsetting the ecological balance that has developed since the planet's creation. Earth's human inhabitants have raided the planet for fuels, used the land, sea and air as rubbish tips, and caused the extinction of over 500 species of animals. For those who believe and care about the future of planet Earth, and who would like to make some contribution, no matter how small, towards its health and management, a variety of conservation work projects offer the opportunity to turn concerns into practical use.

Work can be undertaken on a wide range of tasks: carrying out surveys to determine current population levels, habits or optimum environment of different species; building trails through forests and nature reserves; cleaning polluted rivers, ponds and lakes; stabilising sand dunes; or acting as environmental interpreter in a nature centre.

There are also plenty of opportunities to preserve the built environment, including the restoration of railways, canals and other aspects of our industrial heritage; conserving churches, castles and monuments; renovating stately homes and gardens; rebuilding abandoned hamlets; preserving archaeological remains; and building drystone walls.

Relevant skills are welcome, but not essential, and many projects will include training on particular aspects of conservation work. All tasks involve work which could not be achieved without volunteer assistance. The projects are normally undertaken during the summer months, though opportunities exist at other times, and sometimes all year round. Basic accommodation is provided in church or village halls, schools, farm buildings or hostels, depending on the situation. Food is usually provided on a self-catering basis, with volunteers taking it in turns to cook. Volunteers contribute towards the cost of food and pay their own travel costs. Work can be strenuous; all volunteers should be fit and are strongly advised to have an anti-tetanus injection before joining any project.

Some of the organisations listed below have a local group network, where, for example, volunteers can get involved in weekend conservation projects taking place in their locality.

The British Trust for Conservation Volunteers, 36 St Mary's Street, Wallingford, Oxfordshire OX10 0EU ✆ Wallingford (0491) 39766 is a charity promoting practical conservation work by volunteers and organises numerous working holidays throughout England, Wales and Northern Ireland. BTCV also cooperate with a number of conservation organisations overseas during the summer to offer places for volunteers on international projects.

The Scottish Conservation Projects Trust, Balallan House, 24 Allan Park, Stirling, FK8 2QG ✆ Stirling (0786) 79697 is a charitable trust promoting the involvement of people in improving the quality of Scotland's environment. Projects are organised throughout Scotland, including the Western Isles, Orkney and Shetland.

National Trust Acorn Projects, Volunteer Unit, PO Box 12, Westbury, Wiltshire BA13 4NA ✆ Westbury (0373) 826826 offer the opportunity to carry out conservation work on National Trust properties throughout England, Wales and Northern Ireland, including houses and gardens, parks and estates, mountains, moors, coastline, farms and nature reserves.

National Trust for Scotland Thistle Camps, 5 Charlotte Square, Edinburgh EH2 4DU ✆ 031-226 5922 ext 257 are residential voluntary work projects organised by the

National Trust for Scotland to help in the conservation and practical management of properties in the care of the Trust.

Earthwatch Europe, Belsyre Court, 57 Woodstock Road, Oxford OX2 6HU ✆ Oxford (0865) 311600 aims to support field research in a wide range of disciplines including archaeology, ornithology, animal behaviour, nature conservation and ecology, giving support to researchers as a grant and in the form of volunteer assistance. Members can take part in expeditions running world-wide, but are expected to share the cost of the expedition and pay their own travel expenses.

COUNTRIES   INDEX

PROJECTS INDEX

ORGANISATIONS INDEX

REPORT FORM

Up-to-date reports enable us to improve the accuracy and standard of information in our guidebooks, and monitor the opportunities available. It would be appreciated if, after a period of voluntary service, volunteers could complete this form and return it to the Information, Print & Design Unit, Central Bureau for Educational Visits and Exchanges, Seymour Mews House, Seymour Mews, London W1H 9PE. **All reports will be treated in strict confidence.**

Name and address of volunteer-sending agency

When did you work for them, and for how long?

Which country/area?

What type of work was involved?

How efficient were the agency in arranging the placement?

How adequately were you occupied during the assignment?

What sort of orientation or training was provided? Do you think it was adequate?

PLEASE TURN OVER

What was the relationship between the organisation you were working for and the local people?

Do you think that volunteers are really needed on the project?

What sort of help or advice was given to you once the assignment had finished?

Would you recommend this volunteer opportunity?

Please feel free to send a covering letter with any further comments you may have

Name

Address

Age   Signed   Date